AF616657

Henry Smith: England's Silver-Tongued Preacher

HENRY SMITH

HENRY SMITH:

England's Silver-Tongued Preacher

R. B. JENKINS

ISBN 0-86554-077-2

All books published by Mercer University Press are produced on acid-free paper that exceeds the minimum standards set by the National Historical Publications and Records Commission.

Library of Congress Cataloging in Publication Data

Jenkins, Ronald B., 1941-

Henry Smith: England's silver-tongued preacher.

Bibliography: p. 121.

Includes index.

1. Smith, Henry, 1550?-1591. 2. Preaching—England—History—16th century. I. Title.

BX9339.S62J46 1983 251'.0092'4 83-878

ISBN 0-86554-077-2

Table of Contents

Dedication

to

Giles Yeomans Newton

ἀρίστου καὶ ἄλλως

φρουιμωτάτου καὶ δικαιοτάτου

Introduction

ALTHOUGH literary and ecclesiastical historians regard Henry Smith as the most popular Puritan preacher of the Elizabethan era, they have neither thoroughly examined his life nor systematically considered his sermons in the context of sixteenth-century ecclesiastical history. This present study attempts to do both. Chapter 1 contains the known facts of Smith's life; chapter 2 explores the chief controversies of the English church in order to reveal the state of preaching in the sixteenth century and Smith's own theological position in that context; and chapter 3 investigates in detail Smith's sermons themselves.

No comprehensive biography of Henry Smith exists. The fullest *Life* is that which Bishop Thomas Fuller attached to his 1675 edition of the collected sermons; it consists of fewer than four pages. When Fuller's edition was reissued by Thomas Smith in 1866 in Nichol's Series of Standard Divines, the editor added eleven pages of notes in which he clarified and supplemented some of the facts Fuller had recorded.

Thompson Cooper, one of the compilers of *Athenae Cantabrigienses,* contributed to that work a three-page biographical sketch of Henry Smith, accompanied by a list of his sermons. Cooper also wrote the two-page entry on Smith in *The Dictionary of National*

Biography. Almost all scholars have turned to the latter source for the facts of Henry Smith's life. After the work of Fuller and Cooper, critics of the Puritan movement have contributed few important facts to Smith's biography.

No biographer, including Cooper, has drawn thoroughly upon John Nichols's account of the Smith family in *The History and Antiquities of the County of Leicester.* Containing detailed information on many of the Smiths of Leicestershire, these county records permit one to see Henry Smith in the proper perspective of his family, his country, and his age. Also of importance is William Burton's *Description of Leicester Shire, Containing Matters of Antiquitye, Historye, Armorye, and Genealogy.*

The sources for a study of Henry Smith's life are to be found only in the collections of large research libraries. Thus, writers on Smith have been generally restricted to one source, namely, Thompson Cooper's two pages in *The Dictionary of National Biography,* which is essentially a restatement of his earlier account of Smith in *Athenae Cantabrigienses.* The biographical study that constitutes chapter 1 of the present work has had frequent recourse to Nichols's *History* and to Burton's *Description of Leicester Shire,* as well as to later materials. Its aim is to bring together all the known facts of Henry Smith's life. No source, when known, has been left unexamined; no fact, when pertinent, has gone unmentioned. Still, the facts are few and often contradictory; but they are at least together now under one cover, making them readily accessible to the interested reader.

A fuller appreciation of Smith is made possible by regarding him and his work in the cultural context in which he lived and preached. Hence, chapter 2 discusses some of the important religious issues of the sixteenth century in order to reveal the state of preaching during Smith's lifetime and to illuminate his own position in the English church. In the Elizabethan age, preaching itself became an issue. Frequently, the pulpit resembled a political platform where issues of state usurped the teaching of spiritual doctrine.

Protestants argued among themselves and, whenever the occasion permitted, defamed Catholics. Such discord prevailed that Queen Elizabeth attempted to restore order by prohibiting all but the duly authorized to preach. To obtain a license, one had to subscribe to the Queen's ecclesiastical supremacy, to the lawfulness of the Prayer Book, and to the Thirty-nine Articles. For a time, the more radical Puritans who refused to take the oath were restrained from preaching; soon, however, the order of silence was relaxed, and many of the silenced Puritans regained their pulpits. Gradually the number of trained preachers increased; and, in due course, a large number of highly competent preachers filled the English pulpits.

Until such time, however, Puritan lectureships took on a great importance. Smith's own affiliation with the English church was as a lecturer at St. Clement Danes. Less restricted by ecclesiastical laws and often living under the patronage and protection of important men, lecturers preached with an independence and freedom of expression denied to licensed clergymen of the Church of England. Certainly from 1560 to 1580, lecturers skillfully managed to circumvent most of the restricting mandates of the Church and State. By 1583, however, Archbishop Whitgift had replaced Grindal; under his administration, rigid controls practically eliminated Puritan lectureships.

Controversy also surrounded the interpretation of Holy Scripture. Both Anglicans and Puritans opposed the Catholic manner of interpreting Scripture, favoring, generally, a literal view of the Bible, derived from private reflection. Among Protestants, Scriptural interpretations became as diverse as individual reflection itself. The Puritans, for example, wished to rid the Church of all practices that Scripture did not sanction or require. Anglicans, on the other hand, often regarded such practices as worthy of being retained because they had had the long sanction of tradition. The peace of the Church was further jeopardized as Protestants argued among themselves about the validity of clerical vestments, genuflection, confirmation, the exchange of rings at marriage ceremonies, ecclesiastical titles, and so forth. The denunciation of vestments and titles, of course, was but one step removed from the denunciation of those who wore them; thus began the so-called Admonition Controversy. Thomas Wilcox and John Field's tract, *An Admonition to Parliament*, represented a trend of thinking that Anglicans regarded as highly dangerous; for, as Matthew Hutton, Dean of York Cathedral, observed, such thought was rapidly moving from the condemnation of cap and surplice to the complete overthrow of the established ecclesiastical order itself.

Such concerns dominated many of the pulpits in England during the years Henry Smith preached; a number of his sermons reveal his interest in these issues, as well as his position on them. Smith himself, however, is typical of the Puritans who wanted reform in a deeper sense; they recognized that neither vestments nor bishops were as important as the concepts and doctrines for which they stood.

Chapter 3 examines in detail Smith's sermons themselves. The edition used in this study is Thomas Smith's 1866 collection of the complete sermons, published in two volumes in Nichol's Series of Standard Divines and based on the edition of 1675. The chapter consists of a discussion of Thomas Smith's 1866 edition, a treatment of the bibliographical problems associated with the arrangement of the sermons, a general survey of Smith's subject matter, an examination of topics of special interest in the sermons, a discussion of Smith's sermon forms, a treatment of his sermon styles, and an observation on the harmony of manner and matter in his sermons.

In brief, the present study sets forth the life and accomplishments of Henry Smith, England's "silver-tongued" preacher, so that one may more fully understand and appreciate the man, his work, and the age in which he lived and preached.

CHAPTER 1

Henry Smith's Service to Elizabethan England

THE MOST EXTENSIVE history of the Smith family is John Nichols's account in *The History and Antiquities of the County of Leicester*. On lands once a part of the Anglo-Saxon kingdom of Mercia, in an ancient county in central England, Henry Smith's ancestors flourished. The original family name was Heriz, not Smith. William Heriz, of Withcote, Leicestershire, was first to assume the Smith name and arms sometime during the reign of King Henry VII.[1] Tradition has William taking the name as a stipulation of his inheritance of the Smith manor and property from a relative in Withcote. Neither he nor his descendants, however, relinquished the Heriz arms entirely, as it continued to be emblazoned in the second quarter of the Smith shield.[2]

Henry Smith's ancestral line can be traced to a second William Heriz, a relative of the first, of Wiverton instead of Withcote. During his lifetime this William Heriz (Smith) was lord of extensive lands "pleasantly situated in the Eastern extremity of the county," in the deanery of Farmland Hundred. According to Nichols,

---

[1]John Nichols, *The History and Antiquities of the County of Leicester* (London, 1795), 2:1:182.

[2]Ibid.

> Withcote was long since divided into two manors; one of which, called *Ashbye's Manor,* having continued for several generations in that family, was [about the time of] Henry VII [1492], given by *William Ashby* . . . to *William Smith,* alias *Heriz,* with *Catharine Ashby* (his daughter) in marriage. The other (formerly called *the King's Manor*) was in 1462 granted by king Henry IV to *John de Dounton* for his life; and was afterwards purchased by the before-mentioned *William Smith,* alias Heriz, a younger branch of the antient [*sic*] family of Heriz, of Wiverton.[3]

Smith's house was "one of the fairest houses in Leicestershire"; and his orchards, gardens, and pasture lands were among the finest anywhere.[4] Before his death in 1512, William began construction of Withcote Church. This vast project was finally completed by Catharine's second husband, Roger Ratcliffe. Nichols's description of the church is an interesting record of the achievments of Henry Smith's great-grandparents. He writes:

> This beautiful little fabrick, resembling an elegant college chapel, is adorned with large pinacles [*sic*], very perfect Gothic; richly embossed and crosses at the top. . . . In the centre pinnacle, at the West end, is one small bell. The inside is extremely neat; the floor very compact and clean; free-stone, and small square black tiles. The roof is painted; and the windows curiously adorned with the portraitures of prophets and apostles in coloured glass; which have been much damaged, and some of them imperfectly put together with fragments. Under them are the arms of . . . *William Smith, Roger Ratcliffe,* and *Katharine Ashby* widow of them both; and of *John Smith* (son and heir of the said *William*) and *Dorothy* his wife; which are also cut in stone at the upper end of the chancel. The arms of *Ratcliffe* are cut in stone, both on the North and South doors, on a shield. On the North door also are those *Ashby* . . . ; and on the South those of *Smith.*[5]

From Nichols's description of Withcote Church, and from other records, we learn that Henry Smith's grandparents were John

---

[3]Ibid., p. 387.

[4]Ibid.

[5]Ibid., p. 392.

and Dorothy Smith. Dorothy was the daughter of Sir Richard Cave, of Northampton. Like Catharine, Dorothy survived her husband and married a second time, becoming the wife of Sir Henry Poole, a knight of Rhodes. Roger, the eldest of John's ten sons, succeeded to the lordship of Withcote when his father died, but he sold Withcote to his brother Ambrose about 1575, and Ambrose proceeded to become a man of considerable wealth as silk merchant to Queen Elizabeth. Ambrose's daughter, Mrs. Dorothy Barneham, is one of Henry Smith's more notable first cousins. Of her Nichols writes:

> The history of Mrs. Barneham . . . is worth preserving. In a MS life of her second husband, we are told that he met with a beautiful young widow in London, and a great fortune, being the daughter of Mr. Humphrey [a mistake for *Ambrose*] Smith of Cheapside, silkman or mercer to Q. Elizabeth, of an antient family in Leicestershire. She had been before married to Benedict Barneham, esq., an alderman of London, who left her a very rich widow; and that consideration, together with her youth and beauty, made it impossible for her to escape the addresses even of the greatest persons about the Court: but sir John was the only happy man who knew how to gain her. . . . This lady had by her first husband (the alderman) four daughters, who were very young when they lost their father, and therefore needed a faithful friend to manage and improve their fortunes; in which trust sir John acquitted himself so honourably, that they had 10,000 pounds each, for their portion, when they came to marry; an immense sum in those days. One of these ladies was wedded to lord Audley; another to sir Francis Bacon, lord viscount St. Albans; a third to William Constable. . . . By sir John Parkington she had one son, John, and two daughters; Mary, the youngest, was wife of sir Robert Brook . . . ; and Anne, the eldest, married sir Humphry Ferrers . . . and surviving him, was afterwards the second wife of Philip Stanhope, earl of Chesterfield. She had by him one son, Alexander, father to James, the first earl of Stanhope.[6]

Such accounts of Henry Smith's family indicate its secure social position in the Elizabethan and earlier ages. Not all of Henry's uncles were as fortunate as Ambrose, nor were all his cousins as distinguished as Mrs. Barneham; of Henry's two brothers, James and

---

[6]Ibid., pp. 388-89.

Roger, almost nothing is known about the former, but a number of facts about Roger and his family are preserved. Nichols writes that Roger left Husbands Bosworth and moved to the town of Edmondthorpe, where "he lived in great consideration, and universally respected, till the age of 84, when he died, in 1655, and is buried under a handsome monument in Edmondthorpe Church."[7] In 1620, Roger obtained from Sir Henry Berkeley "the manor and lordship of Edmondthorpe, to which there then belonged a court-leet, free-warren, a clerk of the market, waits, strays, and felons goods by ancient charters."[8] The year following the purchase, Roger built a house which he named New Hall, "a little more distant from the church than the antient mansion-house stood, which was on a piece of ground, now within the park, called the Churchyard-close."[9] Nichols describes Roger's house and property thus:

> The park, in which the house is built, borders on the village, and partakes of some pleasing appendages; the deer, some swells of earth, and clumps of trees, are subjects for the pencil, and lively objects for the eye of him who contemplates on the ways of Nature. The site is rather low and obscured; consequently the views hence are not extensive. The rooms possess a pleasing neatness, though they afford but little to admire of the works of artists. The house originally surrounded a court, which has been converted into two very commodious staircases, one of which possesses grandeur. The dwelling, and the adjacent grounds, are watered by a natural stream, which takes its rise from Woodwell-head, a noted fox-cover, in the extremity of the lordship, of which there is a picturesque view from the South front.[10]

In addition to the records pertaining to Roger's house and lands, monumental inscriptions in the Edmondthorpe Church give his dates of birth and death and a few notable facts about his life. Nichols writes:

---

[7]Ibid., p. 183.

[8]Ibid., p. 176.

[9]Ibid.

[10]Ibid., p. 177.

> At the upper end of the South aisle, in a part now inclosed by way of chapel, is a large monument of alabaster and black marble . . . being a tomb whereon is a lady lying at length on her side, her arm resting on a pillow. On another floor higher, a second lady in like manner; and higher, on the third, a man lying flat, with a Bible in his hand, and his left on his breast. All these are large as life; and the whole finishes in a compass, or arch, bearing quarterly [the Smith arms] . . . ; and below, in the hollow of the arch, above the figures, this inscription:
>
>> Here lieth the grave and religious sir Roger Smith, knight, lord of this manor, and formerly one of the justices of this county; whose worthy parts are adorned with the worth of his descent; whose greate grandfather William Smith, alias Herez, descended of the ancient family of Herez, of Wiverton, in the county of Nottingham, is by females passinge throw the names of Ashby, Burdet, Zouch, and Conan Duke of Brittaine, descended from Henry the First, Kinge of England. He dyed anno domini 1655, aged eighty-fower yeares.[11]

Roger's two wives, with memorial inscriptions of their own, lie with him in the Edmondthorpe Church. These facts and records indicate that in the town of Edmondthorpe, in the extreme eastern edge of the county of Leicester, Henry Smith's brother and descendants achieved their measure of worldly renown and that Henry was descended from a long line of securely established men and women who, in their own way, left their impact upon their world. Like them, Henry carried on that tradition and like them, too, in his own way.

Most authorities agree with Charles Henry and Thompson Cooper that Henry Smith was born "in or about 1560 at Withcote in Leicestershire, the seat of his grandfather, John Smith, esq.,"[12]

---

[11]Ibid., p. 180.

[12]Charles Henry Cooper and Thompson Cooper, comps., *Athenae Cantabrigienses* (Cambridge: Deighton, Bell, and Co., 1861), 2:103.

who died in 1546.[13] He was the eldest son and heir of Erasmus Smith. According to Thompson Cooper, author of the Smith entry in *The Dictionary of National Biography*, Henry's mother was Erasmus's first wife, "the widow of one Wye and daughter of one Baiard";[14] but in *Athenae Cantabrigienses* Cooper declares her to be the daughter of Lydd,[15] perhaps a typographical error for Bydd; for Thomas Fuller had called her Miss Bydd in his *Life of Mr. Henry Smith*, prefixed to his edition of Smith's sermons.[16] Henry's stepmother was Margaret Cecil, sister of the famous Lord Burghley and widow of Roger Cave.[17]

Records attest that Henry was admitted a Fellow-Commoner of Queen's College, Cambridge, on 17 July 1573, but evidence suggests he did not matriculate or remain long at Queen's.[18] Two years later, when Henry was about fifteen years old, he was matriculated at Oxford as a member of Lincoln College.[19] It is questionable whether Smith took the Bachelor of Arts degree at Lincoln. Anthony Wood concludes that the Henry Smith who received the Degree of Bachelor of Arts in 1574 is not likely to be the Henry who was matriculated in Lincoln College the year before. Wood writes that Smith was not long in residence at Lincoln College, but was absent, "having some Ecclesiastical employment conferred upon him."[20] Cooper, in *Athenae Cantabrigienses*, also

---

[13]Sir Leslie Stephen and Sir Sidney Lee, eds., *The Dictionary of National Biography* (Oxford: Oxford University Press, 1949-50), 18:456.

[14]Ibid.

[15]Cooper and Cooper, *Athenae Cantabrigienses*, 2:103.

[16]Thomas Smith, ed., *The Works of Henry Smith*, 2 vols. (Edinburgh: James Nichol, 1866), 1:x.

[17]Stephen and Lee, *DNB*, 18:456.

[18]Cooper and Cooper, *Athenae Cantabrigienses*, 2:103.

[19]Anthony Wood, comp., *Athenae Oxonienses*, 2nd ed. (London: Printed for R. Knaplock, D. Midwinter, and J. Tonson, 1721), 1:263.

[20]Ibid.

concludes that "[f]or some reason with which we are not acquainted, [Smith's] father refused to allow him to spend much time in the university, on leaving which he lived and followed his studies with Richard Greenham, the pious rector of Dry Drayton in Cambridgeshire, sometime fellow of Pembroke Hall."[21]

Although uncertain about Smith's Bachelor of Arts degree, Wood writes that "at length, in 1583, [Smith] did take the Degree of Master of Arts, as a Member of *Hart-hall*, being then esteemed the Miracle and Wonder of his Age, for his prodigious Memory, and for his fluent, eloquent, and practical way of preaching."[22] The Coopers doubt that Smith received the Master of Arts degree because he never referred to himself as Master, nor was so styled by others. However, Bishop Fuller, in his short *Life* of Smith, writes:

> As to his not calling himself Master of Arts, or being so called by others, we are perfectly aware that the Messrs. Coopers are abundantly more conversant with English university customs than we are; but we suspect that the designation '*Mr* Henry Smith,' by which he is generally noted on the title pages of his separate sermons, is equivalent to 'Henry Smith, M.A.' We have had occasion to examine many Scottish lists of the 16th century, and have come to the conclusion that in them the prefix *Mr* or *Maister* is usually employed to designate master of arts. We do not know whether the same usage prevailed in England, but we think it highly probable.[23]

Thus, whether or not Smith was ever awarded the Master of Arts degree remains uncertain. Richard Greenham remarked to Lord Burghley that Smith left the university before his gifts matured, implying that Smith never received the M.A. degree; but Greenham's remark suggests only that Smith had not received the degree at the time of his letter to Lord Burghley.

---

[21]Cooper and Cooper, *Athenae Cantabrigienses*, 2:103.

[22]Wood, *Athenae Oxonienses*, 1:263.

[23]Thomas Smith, *The Works of Henry Smith*, 1:xii.

With or without a degree, however, it is certain that Smith, as eldest son, was first in line to inherit his father's estate. Thompson Cooper writes that although Smith "was heir-apparent to a large patrimony, he resolved to enter the ministry,"[24] as if to enter the ministry and to receive a large patrimony were incompatible. Bishop Fuller, in his *Life*, writes thus of Smith's patrimony and of his resolution to devote himself to the ministry:

> [Smith] was none of those who in the university wither the stalk they grow on, and, out of idleness, bury their talents in the ground . . . , but he resolved to improve his utmost in the ministerial calling, for the glory of God and converting souls. Here he triumphed over that temptation wherewith many had been overcome. Plentiful was his estate for the present, and for the future he was heir-apparent to a large patrimony. Preaching was presented unto him by some as fit for the refuge of a younger brother, not for the choice of an heir: his rich relations might better advantage him in the lucrative profession of the law. But he was so far from falling or stumbling, that he did not stop at these carnal considerations, but easily trampled upon them.[25]

Thomas Smith, who edited Fuller's edition of Smith's sermons in 1866, gives the real reason why Smith never succeeded to his father's patrimony and why it passed instead to his younger brother Roger: Smith predeceased his father. Had he lived, he would have inherited the patrimony which was his due; for, as Thomas Smith points out, "We have no reason to think that a [P]rotestant clergyman in those days was precluded from the possession of landed property."[26]

Those who see Smith as willingly turning over the great legacy that was rightfully his to a younger brother in order to devote himself to the hard task of building up treasures in heaven are at least partly right; for Smith was, from all indications, always more

---

[24]Stephen and Lee, *DNB*, 18:456.

[25]Thomas Smith, *The Works of Henry Smith*, 1:vii-viii.

[26]Ibid., xiii.

interested in his spiritual than in his material well-being. He extended his spiritual concerns to others as well as to himself; and if he did, in fact, leave the university before taking a degree, he might well have done so in order to begin his active ministry.

Perhaps Smith's university training and his entry into the ministry overlap; for having left Lincoln College for ecclesiastical employment, he may have returned later for further training. Thomas Smith, in his supplementary notes to Fuller's *Life* of Smith, speculates that, although no positive evidence exists regarding Smith's ecclesiastical ties, he probably procured a curacy in Leicestershire and lived "at his father's house at Market Bosworth's, doing duty for the clergyman of the parish, when he was applied to by the 'Lords Justices,' at the instigation, we presume, of his uncle, Bryant Cave, the high sheriff of the county, to take [Robert] Dickons in hand."[27] Fuller, in *The Church History of Britain*, writes:

> This year [1582] Robert Dickons, a Leicestershire youth, but, it seems, apprentice at Mansell in Nottinghamshire, having parts and pregnancy above his age and profession, arrived at such a height of profaneness, as not only to pretend to visions, but account himself Elijah, sent from God to perfect some defects in the prophecy of Malachi. But by God's blessing on the endeavors of Mr. Henry Smith . . . this heretic was reclaimed, renouncing his blasphemies by subscription under his own hand.[28]

Upon the occasion of Dickons's conversion, Smith preached a sermon later published under the title of "The Lost Sheep Is Found." Whether or not Smith was at that time affiliated with the Husbands Bosworth Church, which was in his father's patronage, is not known.

By this time Henry had apparently decided to abandon forever all other possible careers. Bishop Fuller records that his rich relatives

---

[27]Benjamin Brook, *The Lives of the Puritans* (London: Printed for James Black, 1813), 2:108.

[28]Thomas Fuller, *The Church History of Britian*, ed. J. S. Brewer, 6 vols. (Oxford: Oxford University Press, 1845), 5:7-8.

had attempted to persuade him to study law, a profession admirably suited to one who at any moment might inherit a large fortune. He also had open to him the career of poet, which he apparently practiced for a short time. None of his poems and only a few of his epigrams survive to suggest the merit of his poetic ability. Smith was also proficient in Latin, for he turned the *Microcosmographia* into Latin sapphics. Joshua Sylvester's English translation of Smith's *Microcosmographia* is extant and is usually included as part of the Smith canon. Although no critical appraisal can now be made of his poetic ability, we do have an encomium on his verse by Thomas Nashe. Nashe writes:

> Nor is Poetrie an Arte whereof there is no vse in a mans whole lyfe, but to describe discontented thoughts and youthful desires: for there is no studie, but it dooth illustrate and beautifie. How admirablie shine those Divines above the common mediocritie, that haue tasted the sweete springs of Parnassus! Siluer-tongu'd *Smith*, whose well tun'd stile hath made thy death the generall teares of the Muses, queintlie couldst thou deuise heauenly Ditties to *Apolloes* Lute, and teach stately verse to trip it as smoothly as if Ouid and thou had but one soule. Hence alone did it proceed, that thow wert such a plausible pulpit man, that before thou entredst into the rough waies of Theologie, thou refinedst, preparedst, and purifidest thy minde with sweete Poetrie. If a simple mans censure may be admitted to speake in such an open Theater of opinion, I neuer saw aboundant reading better mixt with delight, or sentences which no man can challenge or prophane affectation, sounding more melodious to the eare or piercing more deepe to the heart.[29]

Forsaking all other careers, Smith devoted himself completely to the Church. A Puritan himself, Smith's antiepiscopal leanings were strengthened when he continued his studies with Richard Greenham about 1576. The pious Greenham had fallen under the influence of Puritan doctrine while he was at Pembroke Hall, which

---

[29]Ronald B. McKerrow, ed., *The Works of Thomas Nashe*, reprinted from the original edition with corrections and supplementary notes by F. P. Wilson, 5 vols. (Oxford: Basil Blackwell, 1958), 4:192-93.

was noted for its antiepiscopal teachings and had produced such martyrs as Nicholas Ridley and John Rogers. Greenham, no doubt, took his share of the Puritan indoctrination with him when he moved to the rectory of Dry Drayton, some three miles from Cambridge. But Greenham was no extremist; and, ultimately, when the Cartwrights, Traverses, and Wilcoxes failed in their efforts to refashion the Church of England according to the Genevan model, men like Greenham and Smith provided an alternate outlet for Puritan energies, for they believed that "a reform of individuals was possible, if not a reform of churches."[30]

Under Greenham's guidance Smith forged the anchors of his own future ministry, learning moderation, restraint, and total dedication, not only from Greenham but also from Greenham's son-in-law, John Dod, and from others who frequented the Dry Drayton rectory and stimulated its inhabitants with lively and intelligent conversation. Greenham was also instrumental in procuring for Smith the lectureship at St. Clement Danes. The fullest account of that appointment is found in John Strype's *Historical Collections of the Life and Acts of the Right Reverend Father in God, John Aylmer*; Strype writes:

> Mr. Henry Smith, an eloquent and witty man, had the last year, *viz.* 1587, become Reader or Lecturer at St. Clement Danes without Temple-Bar, at the desire of the parishioners, and by the favour of the Lord Treasurer [Burghley], who dwelt in the said parish, and yielded contribution to him. This is the Smith whose sermons have been a common family book even to this day, and often reprinted.... The Lord Treasurer took notice of the man, especially when he put in for the preacher's place in the parish of St. Clement's. Therefore he obtained a testimonial and character from Greenham to the said Lord. . . . [Greenham wrote] "That he would not speak of his human literature, whereof he supposed Smith himself had given him [the Lord Treasurer] some small token, (he meant, I suppose, by a sermon preached before him), but he had perceived him to

[30]Everett H. Emerson, *English Puritanism from John Hooper to John Milton* (Durham NC: Duke University Press, 1968), p. 146.

> have been well exercised in the holy Scriptures, religious and devout in mind, moderate and sober in opinions and affection, discreet and temperate in his behaviour, industrious in his studies and affairs, and, as he hoped, of an humble spirit and upright heart, joined with the fervent zeal of the glory of God and health of souls. Which mixture of God's gifts put him in hopes, that God hereafter might be much glorified in him."[31]

Smith remained at St. Clement's only one year before he was suspended by Archbishop Whitgift on the recommendation of Bishop Aylmer, silencing "for a while," according to J. B. Marsden, "probably the most eloquent preacher in Europe."[32] Again, the fullest account of the suspension and subsequent reinstatement occurs in Strype's *Life and Acts of John Aylmer*:

> In short he [Henry Smith] was permitted to read (that is, to preach a lecture) at St. Clement's, where one [William] Harewood was now Parson. But the next year, being the year 1588, our Bishop, being informed that he had spoken in his sermon some words derogatory to the Common Prayer, neither had subscribed the Articles, wherein was contained the approbation of the said book, suspended him from preaching a while. His own case he drew up briefly for the information, it seems, of the Lord Treasurer.[33]

The Bishop of London alleged that Smith was chosen as lecturer by the people of the parish and by Parson Harewood and that he was not officially licensed. Strype gives Smith's answer to these allegations:

> First, touching my calling thither, I was recommended to the parish by certain godly preachers, which had heard me preach in other places in this city; and thereupon accepted of by the parish, and entertained with a stipend raised by voluntary contribution: in which sort they had heretofore entertained others without any such

---

[31]John Strype, *Historical Collections of the Life and Acts of the Right Reverend Father in God, John Aylmer, Lord Bp. of London in the Reign of Queen Elizabeth* (Oxford: The Clarendon Press, 1821), pp. 100-101.

[32]J. B. Marsden, *The History of the Early Puritans from the Reformation to the Opening of the Civil War in 1642* (London: Hamilton, Adams & Co., 1850), p. 178.

[33]Strype, p. 101.

question or exception. Secondly, his Lordship calling me to preach at Paul's Cross never moved any such question to me. Nevertheless, if any error have been committed herein either by me or the parish, through ignorance, our joint desire is to have his Lordship's good allowance and approbation for the exercise of my function in his Lordship's diocese. Touching the second, however, his Lordship hath been informed against me; I never used speech in any of my sermons against the said Book of Common Prayer; whereof the parish doth bear me witness in this supplication to your Lordship. Concerning the third, I refuse not to subscribe to any Articles, which the law of the realm doth require of men of my calling: acknowledging with all humbleness and loyalty her Majesty's sovereignty in all causes, and over all persons within her Highness's dominions; and yielding my full consent to all the Articles of faith and doctrine taught and ratified in this Church, according to a statute in that behalf provided the thirteenth year of her Majesty's reign. And therefore [I] beseech his Lordship not to urge upon me any other subscription than the law of God and the laws positive of this realm do require.[34]

Strype concludes that, whether Smith actually subscribed to the Articles later, he at least came again into the good favor of the Bishop, for he was allowed to continue at this post as lecturer until 1589.[35] Perhaps the Lord Treasurer influenced the reinstatement of Smith; for, as Fuller writes, "he was often the screen who saved Mr. Smith from the scorching, interposing his greatness betwixt him and the anger of some episcopal officers."[36] At any rate, Smith's popularity continued to increase, and in 1589, "upon the dangerous sickness of Harewood the incumbent," writes Strype, "divers of the parish petitioned the Lord Treasurer, that in case he died, Mr. Smith their preacher might succeed him."[37] Even though these men stated

---

[34]Ibid.

[35]See Daniel Neal, *The History of the Puritans* (New York: Harper & Brothers, 1844), for copious evidence regarding the seriousness of ecclesiastical charges and accusations.

[36]Thomas Smith, *The Works of Henry Smith*, 1:viii.

[37]Ibid.

to Burghley that Smith's "preaching, living, and sound doctrine, had done more good among them, than any other that had gone before, or, which they doubted, could follow after,"[38] Smith did not receive the appointment, probably because he himself refused it.

Knowing himself to be in failing health, Smith went into early retirement and died two years later. Although I suggest 1591 as the date of his death, records indicate a possible variation of twenty-two years. My choice of 1591 is the earliest date suggested. Both *The Dictionary of National Biography* and *Athenae Cantabrigienses* cite it. In the latter work, Cooper comments thus on Smith's last days:

> During his sickness, being desirous to do good by writing, he occupied himself in revising his sermons and other works for the press. His collected sermons he dedicated to his kind patron lord Burghley. . . . He died before this collection came from the press, being buried at Husbands Bosworth in his native county. In the register of that parish is this entry: Anno 1591, Henricus Smyth, theologus, filius Erasmi Smyth, armigeri, sepult. fuit 4to. die Julii.[39]

Thomas Nashe's remark that Smith's great abilities "hath made [his] death the generall teares of the Muses" indicates that Smith was dead by the time Nashe's *Pierce Penniless* was published in 1592.

Despite such evidence, however, a number of authorities prefer later dates. For example, Anthony Wood writes that Smith "was in very great renown among Men in fifteen hundred ninety and three; in which Year, if I mistake not, he died, aged thirty-four, but where he was buried, the Register of St. Clements . . . tells us not."[40] Wood does not give any reason for choosing 1593. Bishop Fuller, in *The Church History of Britain*, writes that Henry Smith died about 1600; he cites Henry's brother Roger as the source of that information, stating in a marginal note that he personally had been

[38]Ibid., p. 103.

[39]Cooper and Cooper, *Athenae Cantabrigienses*, 2:103.

[40]Wood, *Athenae Oxonienses*, 1:263.

so informed by Sir Roger himself.[41] Strangely, however, when Fuller later wrote his *Life* of Smith, he does not mention this very authoritative source at all, but repeats his efforts to discover from the old men of St. Clement Danes the date and cause of Smith's death. He recounts his search as follows:

> Some fifteen years since I consulted the *Jesses*, I mean such who passed for old men in the parish of St. Clement Danes, but could recover very little of them, either of the time or manner of his death, save that they conceived his disease was a consumption. I perused also the church register, and found it silent concerning the date of his death; for which this reason was alleged, that a little before his departure out of this life, he departed the city to have the benefit of country air. But by the exactest proportion of time, his death may be conjectured to have been about the year 1600.[42]

Two remaining sources might be cited for the sake of thoroughness. John George Phillimore, in his *History of England during the Reign of George the Third*, comments on Smith as follows:

> Perhaps as great a master of English prose as ever wrote, is a writer now almost unknown, Henry Smith, who preached at St. Clement Danes, and died certainly before 1609. There are passages in his works equal to those of any English prose writer.[43]

And, finally, Thomas Tanner, in his biographical paragraph on Smith, cites the late date of 1613.[44]

Whatever the date of his death, one fact remains abundantly clear: during his lifetime Henry Smith was an enormously popular

---

[41]Thomas Fuller, *The Church History of Britain*, 5:8.

[42]Thomas Smith, *The Works of Henry Smith*, 1:ix-x. Cf. Benjamin Brook, *The Lives of the Puritans* (London, 1813), 2:111: "He died apparently of a consumption, about the year 1600, aged fifty years."

[43]John George Phillimore, *History of England during the Reign of George the Third* (London: Virtue Brothers & Co., 1863), p. 113.

[44]Thomas Tanner, *Bibliotheca Britannico-Hibernica* (London: William Bowyer, 1748), p. 678.

preacher and achieved great renown at St. Clement Danes. For example, Benjamin Brook, in *The Lives of the Puritans,* writes:

> Henry Smith was a preacher uncommonly followed by persons of piety, especially those of the puritanical party. He was generally esteemed the first preacher in the nation; and, on account of his prodigious memory, and his fluent, eloquent, and practical way of preaching, he was looked upon as the very miracle and wonder of the age. It may be truly said of him, that he was a man peaceable in Israel. For though he scrupled conformity himself, and utterly disapproved the imposition of it on others; still he could live on terms of intimacy with those from whom he dissented. His fame was so great, that he was usually called the *silver-tongued preacher,* as if he was second even to Chrysostom. His church was so crowded with hearers, that persons of quality, as well as others, were frequently obliged to stand in the aisles; and his wonderful dexterity in preaching was such, that, by his solid reasons, he fastened conviction upon the judgments of his auditory; by his apt similitudes, upon their fancies; by his orderly method, upon their memories; and by his close application, upon their consciences.[45]

Not only was Smith's church crowded to overflowing, his sermons were printed in many editions. J. B. Marsden writes that Smith's "sermons and treatises were soon to be found in the hands of every person of taste and piety; they passed through numberless editions; some of them were carried abroad and translated into Latin. They were still admired and read at the close of nearly a century, when Fuller collected and republished them."[46] In an age of great prose, Smith's fifty-six sermons are among the finest. In contrast to many of the Elizabethan sermons, Smith's "are free, to an astonishing degree," writes Marsden, "from the besetting vices of his age—vulgarity, and quaintness and affected learning."[47] Rising above his contemporaries, Smith "was one of the first English preachers who, without submitting to the trammels of a pedantic logic, conveyed, in

---

[45]Benjamin Brook, *The Lives of the Puritans,* 2:111.

[46]J. B. Marsden, *The History of the Early Puritans,* p. 178.

[47]Ibid., p. 179.

language nervous, pure, and beautiful, the most convincing arguments in the most lucid order, and made them the groundwork of fervent and impassioned addresses to the conscience."[48]

Smith was a city preacher, and his church following was largely the London middle class. Like the sermons of most preachers, Smith's catered to the problems and concerns of his audience. His was not a congregation of extremists, nor was he an extremist in his own thinking. Indeed, he opposed those who wished to split the Church. As a city preacher, he had much to say, as George Krapp observes, "against city vices, against the sin of usury, as it was then regarded, against lawyers, against sleeping in church, physical and spiritual, gambling, extravagance in dress and fashion, drunkenness and other crudities of conduct, though it should be said that these topics are only introduced by the way as practical applications of spiritual truths which are more broadly apprehended."[49] Furthermore, Smith's sermons, with their wide appeal to sixteenth-century middle-class congregations, have found sympathetic readers even in our own age. In fact, Sir A. W. Ward and A. R. Waller, in *The Cambridge History of English Literature,* place Smith "alone among Elizabethan preachers . . . with Hooker [to share] the distinction of finding modern readers."[50] Those who are familiar with his sermons know that they have a worth beyond their interest as period pieces. Combining the force of language with the force of thought, they constitute a distinguished corpus of sermons in an age characterized by great preaching and insure that, whenever English sermons are talked of, Henry Smith's will be mentioned with respect and admiration.

---

[48]Ibid.

[49]George Philip Krapp, *The Rise of English Literary Prose* (New York: Frederick Ungar Publishing Co., 1915; republished, 1963), p. 194.

[50]Sir A. W. Ward and A. R. Waller, eds., *The Cambridge History of English Literature,* 15 vols. (Cambridge: Cambridge University Press, 1961), 4:237.

CHAPTER 2

The State of Elizabethan Preaching

To APPRECIATE more fully the importance of Henry Smith's preaching, one must see him and his work in the context of the important religious issues of the sixteenth century. Religious strife, which disrupted the English church during the reigns of Henry VIII, Edward VI, Mary, and Elizabeth, brought about the alteration and, at times, the abolishment of religious practices that tradition and canon law had formed and protected.

The use of Latin in worship services, for example, was gradually abolished. Although Thomas Cranmer's English litany of 1544 is the first significant encroachment of the vernacular upon the Latin service, the reign of Edward VI saw further inroads, for in his Royal Chapel liturgical precedents were set and then emulated throughout the kindgom. By 4 November 1547, at the opening mass of Parliament, the *Gloria in excelsis, Credo,* and *Agnus Dei* were rendered for the first time in the vernacular.[1] Less than a year later, on 9 September 1548, Robert Ferrar was consecrated Bishop of the see of St. David's, at which time both the Eucharist and the consecration of the Sacrament were in English.[2] On 21 January

---

[1]Horton Davies, *Worship and Theology in England from Cranmer to Hooker, 1534-1603,* 5 vols. (Princeton NJ: Princeton University Press, 1970), 1:169.

[2]Ibid.

1549, the Act of Uniformity was passed, stressing the need to "draw and make one convenient and meet order, rite, and fashion of common and open prayer and administration."[3] That need was met in one of England's great literary achievements: the *Book of Common Prayer,* the chief unifying element of the Established Church during the reign of Queen Elizabeth.

Although the Prayer Book did not appear until 1549, during the reign of Edward VI, Thomas Cranmer had been thinking of such a work for fifteen years or more, perhaps as early as his first exposure to Lutheran rites in the vernacular during his sojourn in Nürnberg as an ambassador for King Henry VIII. Regarded as a means of unifying the disparate rites then in use throughout England, such as the Uses of Sarum, York, Bangor, and Lincoln, the Prayer Book offered a form of worship in the English tongue for the benefit of the masses who were ignorant of Latin. Before its introduction, the English worship service had been read in Latin to the people, "whiche they understoode not; so that they have heard with theyr eares onely; and their hartes, spirite, and minde, haue not been edified thereby."[4] The *Book of Common Prayer* remedied that deficiency and, in addition to meeting the needs of all the common services, included forms for special services, practically eliminating the use of Ordinals, Pontificals, Breviaries, Processionals, and Missals.[5] So inclusive was the Prayer Book that it attempted to meet the needs of priest and laity alike and to narrow the gap that before had always separated the two.

Despite its virtues, however, the *Book of Common Prayer* was not well received and would likely have sunk into immediate obscurity had the Act of Uniformity not insisted upon its use. Attempting to please everybody, it pleased nobody fully. Catholics

---

[3]Ibid., p. 174.

[4]Ibid., p. 175.

[5]Ibid., pp. 176-77.

were alienated because of its Protestant leanings, and Protestants objected to its popish elements. Not even the mandate of the Crown had sufficient strength to sustain for long the form which appeared in 1549. Cranmer was compelled to revise the *Book of Common Prayer*, and in 1522 he did so. His revision, at the insistence of men like Bucer, Martyr, Gardiner, and Ridley, was strongly Protestant. Horton Davies writes: "It is significant that when the 1549 Book came to be revised, at every point where Gardiner had detected residual Catholicism the words were expunged; even the Canon itself was so rearranged as to exclude the remotest possibility of its being interpreted as a propitiatory sacrifice for the living and the dead."[6] More pleasing to Protestants, but much less so to Catholics, the 1552 Prayer Book was also destined to a short life—a shorter life, in fact, than that of its predecessor. In 1553 when Mary Tudor was on the throne, Cranmer and his most significant achievement fell together.

In 1559, during the reign of Elizabeth, the Prayer Book was again revised, and this edition enjoyed a longer life than both of the other Prayer Books combined, continuing in use until the Restoration version of 1661.[7] With the *Book of Homilies*, which was first

---

[6]Ibid., p. 201.

[7]Cf. Ibid., p. 211: The Elizabethan Prayer Book contained a number of changes from the second Prayer Book of 1552, several of considerable significance: "An additional table of lessons for Sundays, festivals, and holy days was provided. In the Eucharist an attempt at comprehension, and inclusion of the different viewpoints was made, which might be confusing theologically, but which was admirable in its sense of charity. The objective and subjective emphases of the Communion were combined by amalgamating the forms of administration of 1549 and 1552 so that at the delivery of the consecrated bread the words are: 'The body of our Lord Jesus Christ which was geuen for thee, preserue thy body and soule into euerlasting life: and take and eate this, in remembraunce that Christ died for thee, and feed on hym in thy hearte by fayth, wyth thankes geuynge.' The Litany's form was not that of 1552, but was the form used in the Royal Chapel, in which the anti-Papal clause was removed. The infamous black rubric was excised, and, although this had not been hinted at in

issued during Edward's reign and retired from use during Mary's, the Prayer Book assisted in bringing order and stability to the English worship service. Appointed lay readers, by using these two books, could provide the remotest parishes with homiletic sermons devoid of theological controversy, political overtones, and sectarianism, as well as a form of worship enjoyed by the most fully staffed parishes of London. Although the Queen herself regarded them largely as a means of achieving national unity and political expediency, these two religious achievements of the Edwardian period undoubtedly filled a very real need in the Elizabethan age.

As a Protestant, Queen Elizabeth had to establish herself as head of the English church, reversing Queen Mary's placement of it under Roman dominion. To achieve this end, Elizabeth drew upon a tradition of obedience inherent in the Christian religion itself, a tradition that reached over fifteen hundred years into the past and had gathered strength with age, making it possible for the four English monarchs of the sixteenth century to demand obedience and conformity of their subjects as the monarchs themselves altered, as they saw fit, the religious practices of the Church of England.

In this tradition, William Tyndale produced *The Obedience of a Christian Man* during the reign of Elizabeth's father, and Stephen Gardiner offered to King Henry two pamphlets attesting his loyalty: *Si Sedes Illa* and *De Vera Obedientia*. Tyndale and Gardiner are representative of a large number of religious leaders who wrote such pamphlets, urging the people to obey without question their prince's commands. Edward, by means of the *Book of Homilies*, furthered the idea of obedience among his subjects. Elizabeth reissued the Edwardian homilies, charging "all parsons, vicars, and curates, every

---

the Act of Uniformity when the 1559 book appeared, it contained a new rubric ordering the use of the vesture worn in 'the seconde yeare of the reyne of King Edward the VI.' This was intended to cover the use of the Mass vestments. In practice, however, the usual vesture was the surplice, over which was worn a cope in the Queen's Chapel and in some cathedral and collegiate churches, in accordance with the rubric of 1549."

Sunday and holy-day in the year, after the Gospel and Creed . . . to read and declare [them] to their parishioners."[8] After a short instruction on universal order, Discourse 12, entitled "An Exhortation Concerning Good Order and Obedience to Rulers and Magistrates," establishes the prince as the head of the earthly chain of being:

> Almighty God hath created and provided for all things in heaven, upon earth, and in the waters under the earth, in a most excellent and perfect order. In heaven he hath appointed various and distinct ranks of angels and archangels; on earth he hath established princes and kings, and inferior officers and rulers. . . . Again, the different seasons, and all parts of the year, as winter, summer, months, nights, and days, each follow the other, and return in orderly succession. Lastly, *man himself* doth in an especial manner discover the most beautiful *order* in his formation . . . ; some are of *high* estate, as kings, princes, and magistrates; some have a *lower* state allotted them, as subjects and inferiors; these may be again distinguished by different degrees of subordination . . . [as] clergy and laity, husbands and wives, parents and children, rich and poor, masters and servants.[9]

Such discourses aimed, of course, to impress upon the Queen's subjects the utter dependency of one social group upon another,

---

[8]Sir Adam Gordon, ed., *Discourses on Several Subjects; Being the Substances of the Homilies of the Church of England*, 2nd ed. (London: Printed for Ogles, Duncan, and Cochran by S. Gosmell, 1817), 1:xivii xivii. Cf. Alan Fager Herr, *The Elizabethan Sermon: A Survey and a Bibliography* (Dissertation, University of Pennsylvania, 1940), p. 20: "This *Book of Homilies* from which priests and readers read was composed in the reign of Edward VI and was issued in 1547. It contained twelve homilies, the small number of which made repetitions frequent. In the epilogue of the book a second volume was promised and the tentative titles of the homilies were listed. In the convocation of 1562 the bishops decided to provide these promised homilies and they prepared them among themselves. This second volume did not contain all of the homilies proposed by the first volume, such as those against covetousness, envy, anger, and malice, but it did contain others not promised in 1563 with a preface by Bishop Cox containing the Queen's rules governing the use of the homilies. . . . Again in 1569 the six parts of the *Homily Against Rebellion* were added . . . , bringing the total number of homilies to thirty-three."

[9]Ibid., pp. 151-52.

stressing the absolute necessity of order and station if kingdoms and commonwealths were to exist harmoniously; for the homilist argued that "without the blessing of *order*, nothing but abuses, licentious manners, oppressive injustice, sin, and confusion, can be expected."[10]

Homiletic indoctrination, the long tradition of obedience in Christian doctrine, the increasing number of Protestants who favored the prince over the Pope as God's earthly viceroy—all together made it possible for English rulers to alter religious practice to suit their own private views.[11] Not even Elizabeth herself, however, could completely escape or ignore the many subtle pressures exerted upon her by religious zealots who demanded that she, as head of the Church, establish its doctrine only upon Scripture, "The Pure Word of God which alone had sufficient authority, as the expression of the divine will."[12] As Davies points out, "It would

---

[10]Ibid., p. 152.

[11]Cf. Horton Davies, 1:9 "Assuming that there was a general agreement among those who had broken with the Papacy, that a Christian prince was the appropriate instrument to undertake the reformation of the church, there was an equally strong negative conviction that the Popes had so far departed from their evangelical office as not to be in any true sense the successors of Peter. Such was the continuing jeremiad of the Protestant pamphleteers. This contention in the controversy with Rome was effectively if crudely propagated with woodcuts or etchings contrasting the meek Christ riding on a lowly ass into Jerusalem with the proud and pompous Pope donning his triple crown as he was carried in state in the gestatorial chair borne by Italian noblemen." Cf. John Jewel, *An Apology of the Church of England*, ed. J.E. Booty (Ithaca NY, 1963), pp. 130-31: "What one thing (tell me) had Peter ever like unto the Pope, or the Pope like unto Peter? Except peradventure they will say thus: that Peter, when he was at Rome never taught the Gospel, never fed the flock, took away the keys of the kingdom of heaven, hid the treasures of his Lord, sat him down only in his castle in St. John Lateran and pointed out with his finger all the places of purgatory and kinds of punishments, committing some poor souls to be tormented and other some again suddenly releasing thence at his own pleasure, taking money for doing so" (cited in Davies, 1:10).

[12]Ibid., p. 15.

have been impossible to have attacked the international power and authority of the Roman Catholic Church, with its immense prestige and immemorial traditions, unless it was believed that the Scriptures were the very word and expression of the will of God."[13]

Regardless, however, of Puritan demands, the form of worship continued to be more important than preaching throughout Elizabeth's reign. A scarcity of licensed preachers restricted the sermon; some parishes, in fact, heard only prescribed homilies; also, the *Book of Common Prayer* emphasized liturgical form. Against all such odds, the sermon survived. Continental and English Reformers, as well as Catholic Humanists like Fisher, Foxe, Colet, and Collingwood, attempted to rescue it and to restore it to its rightful place in the worship service. While the Catholics rather quietly aided the sermon by preaching, encouraging others to preach, and establishing university professorships to promote the study of Scripture in Greek and Hebrew, the Reformers, both on the Continent and in England, bordered more on what might be called the lunatic fringe, so great was their zeal. Espousing their individual interpretations of Scripture, the radical Puritans used the sermon to scourge the shortcomings of the Established Church.

Regarding these preachers as subversive and disloyal to the Crown, the Queen took drastic measures to silence them. She commanded Grindal, her primate, to instruct his bishops to prohibit all Puritan "prophesying" in their dioceses.[14] In a letter to the Queen on 20 December 1576, the Archbishop refused her command. As a result, he was sequestered for six months to his palace at Lambeth and, in fact, never fully regained his former authority despite appeals on his behalf by the House of Clergy.[15] On 7 May 1577, Queen Elizabeth, bypassing Grindal entirely, issued a command

---

[13]Ibid., p. 13.

[14]Ibid., p. 299.

[15]Ibid.

directly to the individual bishops, attempting to restrict the Puritan "prophesyings" and to keep preachers from using the pulpit to disseminate their own contentious views.[16]

Upon silencing Puritan "prophesyings," the Queen's mandate permitted only licensed clergy to preach. To obtain or retain a license, each clergyman had to subscribe to the Queen's ecclesiastical supremacy, to the lawfulness of the Prayer Book and the Ordinal, and to the Thirty-nine Articles of Religion. The Marian bishops, of course, refused to subscribe to such conditions and, consequently, lost their posts. Their removal depleted the number of learned clergy, and years passed before England enjoyed again an abundance of educated preachers. The scarcity of licensed clergymen prevented some of the remoter parishes from hearing more than four sermons a year, the minimum required by law; but "even at these four

---

[16]The Queen's proclamation is cited from John Strype's *Annals of the Reformation and Establishment of Religion, and Other Various Occurrences in the Church of England, during Queen Elizabeth's Happy Reign* (Oxford: The Clarendon Press, 1824), 1:2:391-92: "The quenes majesty, understanding that there be certain persons, having in times past the office of ministery in the Church, which now do purpose to use their former office in preaching and ministery, and partly have attempted the same; assembling, specially in the city of London, in sondry places, great nomber of people: whereupon riseth amonges the common sort not only unfruteful dispute in matters of religion, but also contention, and occasion to break common quiet: hath therefore, according to the authoritie comitted to her highness, for the quiet governaunce of all maner her subjects, thought it necessary to charge and commaund, like as hereby her highness doth charge and commaund, all maner of her subjects, as well as those that be called to ministery in the Church, as all others, that they do forbear to preach or teach, or to gyve audience to any maner of doctrine or preachyng, other than to the gospels and epistels, commonly called the gospel and the epistel of the day, and to the Ten Commaundements in the vulgar tongue, without exposition or addition of any maner sense or meaning to be applyed or added; or to use any other maner of publick prayer, rite, or ceremony in the Church, but that which is already used, and by law receaved; or the common letany used at this present in her majesty's own chappel, and the Lords Prayer, and the Crede in English; until consultation may be had by parlament, by her majesty, and her three estates of this realme, for the better conciliation and accord of such causes as at this present are moved in

occasions the 1559 *Common Prayer* allowed the preacher to substitute a reading from the *Book of Homilies* for the sermon."[17]

The failure of the Established Church to provide adequate preaching may well have provoked religious extremists to take matters into their own hands. Alan Fager Herr writes:

> The zealots who most wanted preaching were the very ones who had been prohibited to congregate and hear sermons; in this group fell the Brownists, the Puritans, the Barrowists, the Family of the Mount, the Family of Love, the Essentialists, and the Anabaptists. But in spite of threatenings and prohibitions under penalty of law, the forbidden assemblies of these unauthorized sects were held furtively in private houses and isolated fields and woods. These secret meetings were at first merely for prayer and meditation, but gradually they came to be focal points of the agitation for the overthrow of the Established Church.[18]

Gradually the state of preaching improved; the Queen relaxed her prohibition; sermons became more numerous; public sermons, such as those at Paul's Cross, became increasingly popular, and church attendance grew. But, then, church attendance was mandatory. Although Englishmen could still believe largely as they saw fit, they were compelled to attend church services or pay a fine.[19]

---

matters and ceremonies of religion. The true advauncement whereof, to the due honour of Almighty God, the increase of vertue and godlyness, with universal charitie and concord amonges her people, her majestie moost desyreth and meaneth effectually, by all maner of means possible, to procure and to restore to this her realme. Whereunto, as her majestie instantly requireth all her good, faithful, and loving subjects to be assenting and ayding with due obedience; so, if any shall disobediently use themselfes to the breach hereof, her majestie both must and will see the same duely punished, bot for the qualite of thoffence, and for example to all others neglecting her majesties so reasonable commaundement."

[17]A. F. Herr, *The Elizabethan Sermon*, p. 16.

[18]Ibid.

[19]Ibid., p. 13. Cf. *Statutes of the Realm, Anno Primo Reg. Elizabeth*, Chapter 2, Section 14 (London, 1810:22): "And that from and after the said Feast of the Nativity of St. John Baptist next coming, all and ever Person and Persons

As the Established Church increased its ranks, the unorthodox sects improved their own situation, strengthening not only their numbers but also the quality of their preaching. Perhaps the Puritans, more than any other faction, increased their number of highly competent, if not truly great, preachers, including Richard Greenham, Henry Smith, Stephen Egerton, Richard Bancroft, Richard Hooker, and Lancelot Andrewes. As the Puritans increased their ranks, they grew bolder in their efforts to expunge what they considered to be the corruptions of the Church. The more radical sects did not care to work for changes within the established framework but sought to level it and begin anew. Moderate Puritans like Henry Smith and Richard Greenham sought changes within. Their sermons, characterized by piety and humility, are in sharp contrast to the vitriolic outpourings of many of their contemporaries. At great personal peril, the bolder Puritans attacked the Queen herself. In 1569, for example, Edward Dering asserted the minister's prophetic role in a direct charge to Elizabeth:

> If you have prayed in tymes past unto God, to modify your enemies hartes, and to bring their cruell practises to nothing: now that you your selfe are set in safety, be not cruell unto Gods anoynted, and do hys Prophetes no harme. . . . It is true that the Prince must defende the fatherles and wydow, relieve the oppressed, and have no respect of persons in judgement, seeke peace unto hys people,

---

inhabiting Dominions, shall diligently and faithfully, having no lawful or reasonable Excuse to be absent, endeavour themselves to resort to their Parish Church or Chapel accustomed, or upon reasonable Let thereof, to some usual Place where Common Prayer and such Service of God shall be used in such Time of Let, upon every Sunday, and other Days ordained and used to be kept as Holy Days, and then and there to abide orderly and soberly during the Time of Common Prayer, Preaching, or other Service of God there to be used and ministered; upon Pain of Punishment by the Censures of the Church, and also upon Pain that every Person so offending shall forfeit for every such Offense twelve Pence, to be levied by the Churchwardens of the Parish where such Offense shall be done, to the Use of the Poor of the same Parish, of the Goods, Lands and Tenements of such Offenders, by the way of Distress" [cited in A. F. Herr, *The Elizabethan Sermon*, pp. 13-14].

> and gyrd hym selfe with righteousness: But thys is also his deuty, and hys greatest dutye, to be carefull for religion: to mayntayne the gospel: to teach the people knowledge, and builde hys whole governaunce wyth faythfulness.[20]

The milder Puritan like Henry Smith was less harsh, never writing, as John L. Lievsay points out, "with the wild immoderation and scurrility too common in his time."[21] Smith, however, like Dering, had the courage to speak his mind, nor was he awed by princely majesty. In "The Magistrates' Scripture," for example, he writes of kings: "though they judge here, yet they shall be judged hereafter, and give account of their stewardship, how they have governed, and straightway their subjects, how they have obeyed."[22]

Smith had the ability to reprove without insulting, to admonish without forcing, and to correct without debasing: "He disdained railing and invectives, the symptom of a sick wit," Bishop Fuller writes, "and if he chanced to fall on a sharp reproof, he wrapped it up in such pleasing expressions, that the persons concerned therein had their souls divided betwixt love and anger at the hearing thereof."[23] Like all of the Puritan preachers, however, Smith emphasized the importance of the sermon itself as the central part of the worship service. The Puritans referred to those who refrained from preaching and read a homily instead as "dumbe dogges." These preachers, they felt, were committing a grievous error; for had they chosen to do so, they might have routed out sin by following it to its origin; the homily reader did not have that opportunity. Thomas

---

[20]Helen C. White, *Social Criticism in Popular Religious Literature of the Sixteenth Century* (New York: The Macmillian Company, 1944), pp. 181-82.

[21]John L. Lievsay, " 'Silver-tongued Smith', Paragon of Elizabethan Preachers," *The Huntington Library Quarterly* 11 (November 1947): 14.

[22]Thomas Smith, ed., *The Works of Henry Smith* (Edinburgh: James Nichol, 1866), 1:357.

[23]Ibid., 1:viii.

Cartwright, for example, in contrasting the "living" sermon with the homily, wrote:

> For where the preacher is able according to the manifold windings and turnings of sin to wind and turn in with it to the end he may strike it, the homilies are not able to turn neither off the right nor off the left, but to what quarter soever the enemies are retired it must keep the train wherein it was set of the maker.[24]

The living sermon, which they regarded as the chief means by which the unredeemed might receive salvation, was significantly more important than the Prayer Book and the homilies which they viewed as impediments rather than guides to the pilgrim bound for the Celestial City; for the one carried form to a noxious extreme; and the other, designed from the outset to restore peace to the kingdom rather than to the soul, restrained God's word in the pulpits.

One means of providing God's word to congregations was by lectureships; and because Henry Smith performed his clerical duties in that capacity rather than as a preacher, one's understanding of him may be enhanced by noting something of their origin and the distinction that was drawn between a preacher and a lecturer. Although the lectureship is neither peculiarly Elizabethan nor peculiarly Puritan, it came to be associated almost exclusively with both.[25] Such a firm association with the age and with the sect derives

---

[24]Horton Davies, *Worship and Theology in England,* 1:296.

[25]Cf. Paul S. Seaver, *The Puritan Lectureships: The Politics of Religious Dissent 1560-1662* (Stanford CA: Stanford University Press, 1970), p. 73, where the association is drawn between friars and lecturers: "[H]owever obvious the spiritual affinity between the two, it is equally clear that there were institutional differences. The friar belonged to a religious order; the lecturer was usually an ordained priest hired specifically to preach. (Occasionally the lecturer had only deacon's orders, which enabled him to preach but not to administer the sacraments.) The friar was frequently itinerant; the lecturer was usually attached to a particular parish and pulpit. The friar, though he belonged to a mendicant order, did not depend on preaching for his livelihood; the lecturer, particularly if he had no cure, frequently did." Cf. Seaver, p. 74, where the following passage is cited from Frederick Pollock's edition of the *Table Talk of John Selden* (London,

from the especial importance each placed on preaching and from the fact that almost all Elizabethan lectureships were staffed by Puritans. In the face of a growing religious aridity, resulting, in part, from the scarcity of licensed preachers, lecturers fulfilled a vital need as they carried God's word throughout England.

For the strictest Precisians, as the Puritans were sometimes called, the administration of the Church, as prescribed by Holy Writ, consisted of four offices: pastor, doctor, elder, and deacon.[26] Paul Seaver, in *The Puritan Lectureships*, distinguishes their functions:

> The offices of pastor and doctor were distinct and their functions different. The pastor or minister preached, administered the sacraments, and prayed; the doctor or teacher interpreted Scripture in order to expound sound doctrine. Although both preached, their preaching served different ends: "The pastor is to take one course, and the Doctor another, for the one is to direct himself principally to exhort, and the other to attend upon doctrine." Hence, according to the disciplinarian model, the lecturer had a permanent place in the true Church, for the function of the lecturer was the same as that of the doctor or teacher. John Udall, a supporter of Cartwright and Travers, made this point obliquely in arguing that "Cathedral Churches have yet some show thereof [i.e., of the true discipline] left in them, who (besides the bishop) have also one that readeth a lecture in divinity."[27]

Although lectureships sprang up with unusual rapidity during the Elizabethan period, supplying many parishes single-handedly with

---

1927): "At Yarmouth, for example, the Franciscans had provided a daily lecture in their abbey church of St. Nicholas prior to 1538. After the dissolution the priory and appropriate parsonage passed into the hands of the dean and chapter of Norwich Cathedral, and the chapter appointed a curate to officiate. By 1563 the corporation of Yarmouth had begun to supplement the impoverished curate's wages; seven years later the merchant guild purchased the living and set about raising a benevolence with which to hire a 'town preacher.' Subsequently the town secured a series of Puritan lecturers until 1635, when the lecturer, George Burdett, was suspended by the High Commission, and the lectureship lapsed in the face of Laudian opposition."

[26]Paul S. Seaver, *The Puritan Lectureships*, pp. 23-24.

[27]Ibid., p. 24.

the word of God and offering more fortunate parishes additional assistance, it is a mistake to regard them with more esteem than is their due. After all, the lectureship was essentially a hasty and, perhaps in the initial conception, a temporary measure undertaken by the Puritans to fill a specific need. No substantial evidence is available to determine whether these posts were "regarded as more than a temporary expedient, an institution to be employed only until a truly reformed church placed a preaching minister in every parish."[28]

Almost all lectureships were parish lectureships, as every London lectureship was. Their aim was to provide sermons for the local congregation, not for outsiders; hence, the lecturer depended solely on local support. He was traditionally recruited by the parish vestry when they felt the need for such a clergyman and had the means to secure him. A licensed minister usually provided the candidate for a lectureship with a suitable letter of recommendation. Seaver writes thus of William Bradshaw's appointment to the lectureship at Chatham:

> When the lectureship at Chatham fell vacant, the vestry agreed to refer the matter to Laurence Chaderton, the master of Emmanuel College, who was at the time in Kent. Chaderton recommended William Bradshaw, and after the "piously affected party" in the parish had confirmed the merits of Chaderton's choice, they blocked any attempt to expand the slate of candidates by requesting Chaderton, now back in Cambridge, to make no further suggestions and by urging Bradshaw to make "no delay in coming to them."[29]

Henry Smith received his appointment at St. Clement Danes in a similar manner. Seaver writes:

> The Puritan preacher Henry Smith was elected to the lectureship at St. Clement Danes on the strength of both a recommendation and a further testimonial. "Touching my calling thither," Smith wrote afterwards, "I was recommended to the parish by certain godly

[28]Ibid., p. 23.

[29]Ibid., p. 135.

> preachers, which had heard me preach in other places in this city." At this point, William Cecil, a parishioner and Smith's uncle by marriage, wrote to Smith's former teacher, Richard Greenham, requesting "a testimonial and character." Greenham replied that Smith was "well exercised in the holy Scriptures, religious and devout in mind, moderate and sober in opinions and affections, discreet and temperate in his behavior, industrious in his studies and affairs, and, as he hoped, of an humble spirit and upright heart, joined with the fervent zeal of the glory of God and health of souls." Henry Smith was, in short, a very paragon of Puritan religiosity, although it may be doubted whether any further testimony to his excellence of character was necessary once he had the Lord Treasurer's backing.[30]

Upon being duly appointed to his post, the lecturer remained there so long as he himself wished or until the vestry removed him for some reason.

The lecturer's chief duty was to preach. Usually, he preached for about an hour twice a week—once on Sunday before or immediately after evening prayer and once on a weekday, usually Wednesday afternoon.[31] Most lecture sermons were exegetical; and, "since lecture sermons were more frequent and more regular than other sermons, some preachers made a practice of expounding a series of related texts over a period of several weeks."[32] The lecturer was not bound in his preaching by the same requirements that often limited the official minister. When, for example, the Instructions for Preachers, issued as mandates from Canterbury, attempted to silence the Puritan voice by requiring set prayers to be read, a number of parishes circumvented the decree by employing at a small fee one to read the prayers, as required, shortly before the lecturer came to the pulpit, freeing him, then, to pray whatever prayers he wished and to preach as his conscience directed. Canon 56 of the 1604 Constitution required that lecturers "shall . . .

---

[30]Ibid., pp. 135-36.

[31]Ibid., p. 143.

[32]Ibid.

administer the Sacraments of Baptism, . . . and of the Lord's Supper, in such manner and form . . . as are prescribed by the *Book of Common Prayer.*"[33] Some of the stricter Puritans, those who violently opposed the Prayer Book, refused to conform to the canon and were duly punished or removed from their lectureships. Others found ways to circumvent the canon and still others obeyed it.

Lectureships were financed by funds collected in the local parish. Although preachers of all ranks were poorly paid, lecturers, as one might expect, were paid even less than licensed preachers.[34] The larger London parishes were especially attractive because they offered more substantial stipends to their preachers and lecturers; large congregations were especially important because a lecturer's stipend depended solely upon voluntary contributions.

From 1560 to 1580 Puritan lecturers managed to circumvent the *ex cathedra* mandates of the Anglican bishops, as well as the Queen's own dictates. In 1581, however, Bishop Aylmer convened "a consistory of the London clergy at which inquiries were made concerning not only those who preached without administering the sacraments, but also those who refused to wear the surplice, who referred continuously to their non-preaching brethren as dumb dogs, and who continued to touch on questions of foreign policy in their preaching."[35] By 1583 a careful watch was being made on lecturers to determine that they were properly licensed and properly conforming.[36] The Puritan cause suffered a further blow in 1583

---

[33]Ibid., p. 145.

[34]Ibid., pp. 147-48: As an indication of the general financial condition in London, it has been estimated that "The average value of London rectories rose from about 19 pounds to about 84 pounds a year between 1535 . . . and 1650. . . . Between 1500 and 1640 the cost of living rose approximately 650 per cent." Lectureships paid as little as six pounds a year as late as 1658, while the presiding preacher in the same parish received 120 pounds.

[35]Ibid., p. 212.

[36]Ibid.

when Grindal, who had been sequestered in 1577 by the Queen for his sympathetic support of Puritan "prophesying," retired and was replaced by the orthodox Whitgift. Whitgift proceeded, with the Queen's consent, to draw up a set of articles inimical to the Puritans. Seaver writes:

> All who preached or ministered were required not only, as in the past, to wear the vestments prescribed by Parker's Advertisements and to say service and administer the sacraments at least four times a year, but also to subscribe to three articles before admission to any preferment. The first, which merely affirmed the royal supremacy, was readily acceptable to the Puritans. The third, which stated that everything contained in the Thirty-nine Articles was "agreeable to the word of God," posed no problems so long as it was taken to pertain only to the doctrinal articles authorized by the statute of 1571. But the second article, which stated that the *Book of Common Prayer* and of Ordination "containeth nothing . . . contrary to the word of God, and that the same may be lawfully used," was entirely unacceptable.[37]

The bishops did not slacken in their efforts to achieve uniformity of practice among the preachers, and after 1583 Puritan lecturers in growing numbers retired from the pulpits. The ecclesias-

---

[37]Ibid., p. 213. Among others, Henry Smith was caught between the Scylla and Charybdis of Whitgift and Aylmer. However, he did not suffer in the hard way of many of his fellow lecturers. Seaver summarizes Smith's position thus: "Henry Smith, who gained an immense reputation as a preacher during his four years as lecturer at St. Clement Danes, owed the lifting in 1588 of Aylmer's suspension to the intervention of his uncle by marriage, Lord Burghley, who was at the time a parishioner of St. Clement's. Aylmer had ample reason for objecting to Smith's lecture; first, Smith had been popularly elected by the congregation and was admitted without the bishop's license; second, he was alleged to have preached against the Prayer Book; and third, he had not subscribed. Smith denied the second charge, and his manner of subscribing to the third was so qualified that it made a mockery of Whitgift's intentions. He acknowledged the royal supremacy, omitted all mention of the Prayer Book, and as for the Thirty-nine Articles, yielded his consent only to those on faith and doctrine 'ratified . . . according to a statute.' He concluded by requesting that Aylmer not 'urge upon me any other subscription than the law of God and the laws positive of this realm do require' " (p. 217).

tical historian Peter Heylyn later wrote that the "Puritans and Presbyterians in both kingdoms were brought so low when King James first obtained the Crown of England that they might have been suppressed for ever, without any great danger, if either the king had held the Reins with a constant hand or been more fortunate in the choice of his Ministers."[38] Be that as it may, it is certain that during Elizabeth's reign Whitgift and Aylmer took their toll on Puritan preachers and lecturers; their policies of suppression continued throughout the century; and, increasingly, the road to the pulpit led through the rigid gates of conformity.

However strictly the English church encouraged conformity, it failed to achieve it in one important aspect of Elizabethan preaching, namely, in the interpretation of Holy Scripture. Although both Puritans and Anglicans generally emphasized a literal interpretation of the Bible, on other matters they held widely divergent opinions. Anglicans and Puritans alike opposed the manner of dividing Scripture into four interpretative levels: literal, tropological, allegorical, and anagogical. Unlike Catholics, Protestants regarded the literal level as the most important. Although not a Puritan himself, William Tyndale expresses the Puritan view of Scripture when, in *The Obedience of a Christian Man,* he writes:

> Thou shalt understand, therefore, that the scripture hath but one sense, which is the literal sense. And that literal sense is the root and ground of all, and the anchor that never faileth, whereunto if thou cleave, thou canst never err or go out of the way. Nevertheless, the scripture useth proverbs, similitudes, riddles or allegories, as all other speeches do; but that which the proverb, similitude, riddle, or allegory signifieth, is ever the literal sense, which thou must seek out diligently.[39]

Not all Elizabethan Protestants, however, confined themselves to a literal exegesis. Thomas Becon, for example, believed that both Jews

---

[38]Ibid., p. 219.

[39]J. W. Blench, *Preaching in England in the Late Fifteenth and Sixteenth Centuries* (Oxford: Basil Blackwell, 1964), p. 38.

and Gentiles dwelt in the Universal Church, for he interpreted the ass on which Jesus rode into Jerusalem on Palm Sunday as representative of the Jewish nation and the colt as representative of the Gentiles. John Foxe regarded Samson's conquest of the Philistines as proleptic of Christ's triumph over the powers of darkness. Thomas Holland, Rector of Exeter College, Oxford, "sees in the visit of the Queen of the South to Solomon (1 Kings x) the foreshadowing of the coming of the Gentiles to Christ, while Edwin Sandys . . . follows traditional interpretation in taking the vineyard in the Canticles (for example, Can. ix. 6) as a figure of the Church, and the foxes which destroy the vines (Can. ii. 15) of her enemies. "[40]

Not only do the sermons of the period reflect individual interpretations of Holy Scripture, they also illustrate the principal thrust of Puritan reform throughout the century from vestiary concerns of the mid-century to a full attack on episcopacy in the last quarter of the century.[41]

---

[40]Ibid., pp. 57-62.

[41]Horton Davies, *Worship and Theology in England,* 1:255-93. Cf. pp. 255-57: "In the 1560s Puritanism centered on trivial sartorial and ceremonial issues. Could a sincerely Protestant minister wear the surplice, a garment worn by the sacrificing priests of the Roman Catholic Church, without compromising his faith? Could he legitimately take part in an Anglican liturgy that required him to bow at the reception of the consecrated species in Holy Communion, and thus commit the idolatry of worshipping the created instead of the Creator, to say nothing of seeming to condone the rejected Roman doctrine of Transubstantiation . . . ? When, however, the battle for a more truly Reformed type of worship moved into the seventies, with the Admonition controversy, there was a far more radical criticism of the *Book of Common Prayer,* and a dissatisfaction with episcopacy . . . and with the ecclesiology of the Church of England since it lacked provision for disciplining and purifying the church membership. . . . In 1588 and 1589 the *Marprelate Tracts* "voiced the growing bitterness of the Puritans against the entrenched episcopal establishment. More positively during the same period, Puritan ministers were giving an example of the godliness and learning that was at the heart of Puritanism. Richard Greenham fulfilled an exemplary pastorate at Dry Drayton, Cambridgeshire from 1570 to 1591, where he also taught pastors, including the brilliant Puritan preacher, Henry Smith, Lecturer at St. Clement

Seemingly insignificant, the vestiary controversy, which began about 1561, symbolized the more serious ills of the Church. In that year, the Queen recommended uniformity of dress among the clergy. Archbishop Parker attempted to sway Thomas Sampson, Dean of Christ Church, and Laurence Humphrey, President of Magdalen College, Oxford, to the Queen's point of view, arguing that the surplice and such vestments, long considered signs of popery, "were ordained not as essential to Christian worship but as a means of obtaining that good order which the magistrate must secure in the Church."[42] The Puritans were not convinced. Needing support, Parker requested Cecil, the Queen's Secretary, "to draw up a letter ordering him to enforce uniformity of clerical dress and get the Queen to sign it."[43] Such a command was necessary, he thought, to give his own mandate the strength it needed among the bishops. Although the Queen complied, she discovered that her signature was ineffective in persuading the Puritans to don the surplice.

As the vestiarian controversy proceeded, the Puritans drew into their camp the former Anglican Archdeacon of Hereford and Prebendary of St. Paul's, Robert Crowley. Urged on by Puritan friends, Crowley composed *A Briefe Discourse against the Outwarde Apparell and Ministering Garments of the Popishe Church*, in which he wrote:

> [I]f the Prince shall take in hand to command us to do any of those things which God hath not commanded . . . , we must then refuse to do the thing commanded by the Prince and humbly submit ourselves to suffer the penalty, but in any case not consent to infringe the Christian liberty which is to use things indifferent to edification and not to destruction. . . . And this is not to give example of disobedience . . . but by example to teach true obedience

---

Danes from 1587, and his son-in-law, the long-lived John Dod, whose kindly witticisms were widely quoted."

[42]M. M. Knappen, *Tudor Puritanism: A Chapter in the History of Idealism* (Gloucester MA: Peter Smith, 1963), p. 189.

[43]Ibid., p. 190.

> both to God and also to man. First we obey God, in that both in doing and leaving undone we seek the edification of his church. And then we obey man, in that we do humbly submit ourselves to suffer at man's hand whatsoever punishments man's laws do appoint for our doing or refusing to do at man's commandment.... Our goods, our bodies, and our lives we do with all humble submission yield into the hands of God's officers upon earth: but our consciences we keep unspotted in the sight of Him that shall judge all men.[44]

The Archbishop responded to Crowley's pamphlet with *A Brief Examination for the Tyme of a Certaine Declaration Lately Put in Print,* which incited the Puritans to counterattack. Suddenly and unexpectedly, assistance came to the Puritans from abroad, inspiring many with hope of victory, when Scottish sympathizers "sent to the bishops a general request for leniency in their dealings with the Puritans."[45] Zurich, however, declined to support the Puritans, and loss of that support was fatal. Anglicans and Puritans alike had sought the support of the Swiss divines, Heinrich Bullinger and Rudolph Gualter, both of whom favored the position of the Anglican bishops. The loss of Continental support dealt the deathblow to the Puritan cause. Most of the Puritans submitted gracefully to the defeat, but the more extreme thinkers separated from their passive

---

[44]Ibid., pp. 198-99. Crowley's attitude toward obedience is in the tradition of Augustine and Aquinas. In *The Confessions,* Augustine writes that we ought "unhesitatingly to obey God, the Governor of all His creatures! For as among the authorities of human society the greater authority is obeyed before the lesser, so must God above all" (Cited from Whitney J. Oates, ed., *Basic Writings of Saint Augustine* [New York: Random House, Inc., 1948], 2:37.) Similarly, Aquinas, in *Summa Theologica,* contends that earthly superiors are to be obeyed only to the extent of their authority, which is limited, and he quotes Seneca (*De Beneficiis,* iii) in support of his argument: "It is wrong to suppose that slavery falls upon the whole man: for the better part of him is excepted. His body is subjected and assigned to his masters, but his soul is his own" (*Summa Theologica,* trans., Fathers of the English Dominican Province [New York: Benziger Brothers, Inc., 1947], 2-2, q. 104, a.5.).

[45]Ibid., p. 204.

brethren and, as Separatists, continued the struggle against the Established Church. The less radical Puritans, however sympathetic in spirit, refused to join the Separatists' war. M. M. Knappen, in his *Tudor Puritanism*, writes:

> They sympathized with the aims of their more extreme brethren, but they could not approve of their tactics. To separate from a church sound in doctrine, however corrupt in ceremonies, in their judgment was to destroy the unity of the Protestant forces and eventually to ruin the cause of clerical idealism altogether. It was quite proper to protest from within the ranks against wearing an improper uniform, to use another, and, if that were not allowed, to abandon one's official position. But to step out of the line altogether, raise a band of *condottieri*, and plan a campaign of one's own—that was unthinkable.[46]

Once outside the fold, the Separatists fought to eliminate not only popish vestments but genuflection, confirmation, the exchange of rings at marriage ceremonies, and other practices not required or sanctioned by Scripture; but the Queen and her bishops prevented their making any significant headway. A group of Puritan leaders, notably Thomas Wilcox and John Field, composed a tract in June 1572, entitled *An Admonition to the Parliament*, urging Parliament to purge the Church of incompetent bishops, to allow congregations a voice in the selection of their own preachers, to reinstate the Church's right to excommunicate sinners, and to abolish vestments and other popish symbols. Parliament viewed the Admonition as a threat to the Established Church itself. Matthew Hutton, Dean of York Cathedral, wrote to Cecil, the Queen's secretary:

> [At first] it was but a cap, a surplice, and a tippet; now it is grown to bishops, archbishops, and cathedral churches, to the overthrow of established order, and to the Queen's authority in causes ecclesiastical. These reformers would take the supreme authority in ecclesiastical matters from the prince, and give it unto themselves.[47]

---

[46]Ibid., pp. 213-14.

[47]Everett H. Emerson, *English Puritanism from John Hooper to John Milton* (Durham NC: Duke University Press, 1968), pp. 17-18.

Eventually Field and Wilcox found themselves in Newgate, but the Puritan press that had produced the *Admonition* was undiscovered and soon put forth *An Exhortation to the Bishops To Deal Brotherly with Theyr Brethren* and *A Second Admonition to Parliament.* In 1572 Bishop Whitgift's *Defense of the Answer* appeared, as did Cartwright's *Reply.* The Admonition Controversy finally wore itself out in recrimination.

In the general wear, the preachers were not the only ones to suffer; their congregations did, too. Sermon topics, for instance, became increasingly secular, as preachers ignored the old themes of the Passion, the Resurrection, the Atonement, and the necessity of living a life worthy of the Christian calling, and directed their energies against the corruptions of the English church. Thus, because the Church could not be neatly separated from the state, preachers frequently neglected the principal tenets of the Christian religion in order to thrash out the affairs of the kingdom, devoting more and more attention to the imperfections of this world and less and less to the perfections of the world to come. Spiritually benumbed congregations became increasingly attracted to anything amusing or sensational. Archbishop Sandys writes:

> The preacher is gladly heard of the people, that can carp the magistrates, cut up the ministers, cry out against all order, and set all at liberty. But if he shall reprove their insolency, pride, and vanity, their monstrous apparel, their excessive feasting, their greedy covetousness, their biting usury, their halting hearts, their muttering minds, their friendly words and malicious deeds, they will fall from him then. He is a railer, he doteth, he wanteth discretion.[48]

Bishop Jewel writes in a similar vein:

> Many are so ignorant, they know not what the scriptures are, they know not that there are any scriptures. They call them heretical and new doctrine. Many will believe neither side, whatsoever they allege. Bring they truth, bring they falsehood; teach they Christ,

[48]John Ayre, ed., *The Sermons of Edwin Sandys, D.D.* (Cambridge: Cambridge University Press, 1841), p. 247.

> teach they antichrist; they will believe neither, they have so hardened their hearts. Be the preacher rough or gentle, learned or unlearned, let him use authority of the scriptures, of the doctors, of the councils, of decrees or decretals, of God's law, of man's law, nothing will move them, nothing will please them; because the ministry of God, and thereby God himself, is despised.[49]

Like Sandys and Jewel, Bishop Babington was so frustrated by his hardhearted congregation that he ended one worship service thus: "And Amen say I againe to this Prayer, leaving you now to your liberty to go forwards with other temptations as you will."[50]

A number of Puritans felt the Queen herself remiss in discharging her responsibilities. Archbishop Hutton, for example, reminded her of her obligation to provide the kingdom with a successor, which, as Alan Herr rightly observes, was "a very dangerous thing to do since she never allowed any discussion of the unpalatable fact that even queens grow old and die."[51] John Manningham recorded in his *Diary* the following incident:

> Dr. Rud made a sermon before the Queene upon the text, "I sayd yee are Gods, but you shall all dy like men;" wherein he made such a discourse of death that hir Majestie, when his sermon was ended, said unto him, "Mr. Dr. you have made me a good funerall sermon, I may dye when I will."[52]

However great an honor it might have been to preach before the Queen, it was also a frightening occasion; for one never knew how she would react to the sermon or the preacher. About the only safe topics were the declaration of her absolute sovereignty and a remonstration against any extension of the Bishop of Rome's authority. Since 1563, when Parliament passed an act assuring the Queen

---

[49]John Ayre, ed., *The Works of John Jewel, Bishop of Salisbury* (Cambridge: Cambridge University Press, 1847), 2:1014.

[50]Alan Fager Herr, *The Elizabethan Sermon*, p. 18.

[51]Ibid., p. 38.

[52]John Bruce, ed., *Diary of John Manningham* (Westminster: J. B. Nichols and Sons, 1868), p. 136.

of her full powers over all states and subjects in her dominion, anti-Catholic sermons had been the staple of the English pulpit. The act provided that punishment be administered to any who

> shall by Writing, Cyphering, Printing, Preaching, or Teaching, deed or Act, advisedly and wittingly hold or stand with, to extol, set forth, maintain or defend the Authority, Jurisdiction or Power of the Bishop of Rome, or of his See, heretofore claimed, used or usurped within this Realm.[53]

In an effort to bridle the tongues of vitriolic Puritans, the government itself used the pulpit from time to time to disseminate propaganda. A number of important ministers of the Church assisted civil authority, as is evident in an excerpt from Bishop Grindal's letter to Cecil:

> I pray you let me understand, whether it may be certainly avouched that the king of Navarre, the second Julian, is killed. I intend (God willing) to preach at the cross the next Sunday, and upon occasion offered would peradventure make some mention of God's judgment over him, if the same be true and certain; else not. If there be any other matter which you wish to be uttered there for the present state, I would be pleased to know it in time, if your leisure will serve. God keep you![54]

Another example is found in the Star Chamber's influence on a number of sermons dealing with the execution of the Earl of Essex, whose great popularity the government thought fit to shroud in any opprobrium whatever:

> Order was taken the Sunday following that the preachers at Paul's cross and other churches in London should deliver the same matters from the pulpit, and decry the Earl as a hypocrite, Papist, and confederate with the Pope and King of Spain, to make him King and bring in idolatry.[55]

One must not conclude from these examples, however, that all Elizabethan sermons were contentious or political. Many

---

[53]Herr, p. 57.

[54]Ibid., p. 51.

[55]Ibid., p. 52.

preachers, both Anglicans and Puritans, ignored, insofar as possible, the disagreements within the Church and the pressures of the state and continued to emphasize biblical themes. Henry Smith was one such preacher. Although his sermons do not shy away from controversial topics, they never emphasize them. Unlike the radical Separatists who knew they had a battle to win but forgot they had a duty to perform, the milder dissenters like Smith preached against sin, emphasized forgiveness, and proclaimed the new life in Christ. They dwelt chiefly on what Smith and others referred to as the "state of contentation," which insisted on loyalty to God, to God's earthly viceroy, the Queen, and to God's true church, the Church of England. Their battle was an old one; their dragon, the ancient serpent of Eden; their chief concerns, those that God's ministers had grappled with ever since Christ commissioned the disciples to preach the gospel to all nations. Smith and others of a similar cast of mind strove with the greatest singleness of purpose to reprove sin where they found it and to reform life at its very core, where reformation was most crucial.

In the exercise of their priestly function, Elizabethan preachers employed to their advantage the rhetorical means of style, structure, and form. J. W. Blench writes that preachers usually constructed their sermons according to the rules of one of three prevalent forms: "the 'ancient' form, the new Reformed arrangement of Doctrines and Uses, and the 'modern style' so modified as to approximate to the true classical form with its variations."[56] Particularly popular during the Middle Ages and associated generally with the homilies of the Church Fathers, the ancient form is "without any elaborate scheme of arrangement peculiar to sermons, and consists either of the explication and application of a passage of Scripture (often the Gospel or Epistle of the Day), *secundum ordinem textus*; or of the

[56]Blench, p. 100.

topical treatment of any subject, according to reason and Scripture."[57]

A favorite form among pre-Reformation Catholics, the ancient form is employed in the lectures of Colet on St. Paul's Epistles and in his sermons at St. Paul's; in Taverner's *Postils;* in Edgeworth's sermons on St. Peter's First Epistle; in Bishop Alcock's sermons to the priests and nuns upon their consecration; in William de Melton's sermon to candidates to be ordained, and in Longland's and Fisher's sermons on the Penitential Psalms.[58] Among the early reformers to employ the ancient form are John Bradford and Hugh Latimer, while among the Elizabethans are Becon, George Abbot, John King, Anthony Anderson, Edward Dering, Richard Greenham, and Henry Smith.

A number of sixteenth-century preachers favored the New Reformed Arrangement of Doctrines and Uses. Employed in the Latin commentaries of Musculus (Wolfgang Muesslin, 1497-1563) and by the early reformer John Hooper in his sermons on Jonah, the New Reformed Arrangement of Doctrines and Uses was particularly attractive in the Elizabethan age among the more extreme Puritans.[59] William Perkins, in the *Art of Prophecying,* describes the form thus:

> [T]he preacher is: (1) "to reade the Text distinctly out of the Canonicall Scriptures"; (2) "to give the sense and vnderstanding of it being read, by the Scripture it selfe"; (3) "to collect a few and profitable points of doctrine out of the natvrall sense"; (4) "to apply (if he have the gifte) these doctrines rightly collected to the life and manners of men in a simple and plain speech."[60]

Among Elizabethans to employ the New Reformed Arrangement of Doctrine and Uses, Thomas Cartwright and Edward Topsell are

---

[57]Ibid., pp. 71-72.

[58]Ibid., pp. 74-76.

[59]Ibid., p. 101.

[60]Ibid., pp. 101-102.

particularly noteworthy. Cartwright followed so closely the prescribed form that his sermons are labored and tedious. Topsell managed the form with greater success, alleviating much of the tedium that usually accompanies sermons of this type.[61]

The third sermon form available to sixteenth-century preachers was the "modern" form. Blench describes it as follows:

> [T]he "modern" style consists of the following parts: the Theme; the Exordium or Protheme or Antetheme; the Prayer; the Introduction of the Theme; the Division (with or without Subdivision); and lastly the Discussion. Of these, the Exordium, Protheme or Antetheme may be omitted, while the Introduction of the Theme is not found in later practice.[62]

Among the pre-Reformation Catholics to employ the "modern" sermon form are Stephen Baron, Bishop Richard Fitzjames, and John Fisher; among the Catholics, John de Feckenham, Leonard Pollard, and John Harpesfield. The "modern" form was particularly useful to the Elizabethans. Edmund Grindal, Bishop of London, employed the form in the funeral sermon of Emperor Ferdinand; Richard Hooker adapted it in a number of sermons, as did Thomas Playfere and Henry Smith.[63]

However important the arrangement, or disposition, of a preacher's material, his sermon style was just as important. Elizabethan preachers had three principal styles from which to choose: plain, colloquial, and ornate.

The plain style, which is the simplest and least embellished of the three, is characterized by the use of few *exempla*, or illustrations, and by only the rarest use of rhetorical schemata, or artificial word patterns.[64] Preachers like Fitzjames, Baron, Colet, Taverner, Tun-

---

[61]Ibid., p. 102.

[62]Ibid., pp. 72-73.

[63]Ibid., pp. 102-11.

[64]Ibid., p. 113. Note also that Blench defines *exemplum* as follows: "The word *exemplum* itself is a generic term, and includes the 'figure' which is a simile

stall, William Chedsey, Cuthbert Scott, and Thomas Leaver employed the plain style to advantage. Although not so popular during Mary's reign, it was used by John de Feckenham, Edmund Bonner, Hugh Glasier, and Reginald Pole.[65] Quite popular during Elizabeth's reign, the plain style itself developed three forms: "first an extremely bare and austere form; secondly a less colourless form, employing tropes but not schemata; and thirdly, a moderately decorated form, employing tropes, and occasionally schemata also."[66] Representatives of the plainest of plain style are Bartimaeus Andrewes, John Stockwood, William Perkins, Laurence Chaderton, Stephen Egerton, William Fulke, George Gifford, and Hugh Roberts.[67] The second form of plain style, characterized by tropes and a few schemata, was employed by Thomas Cartwright, Thomas Gybson, Anthony Anderson, and Richard Maddoxe.[68] The third and most elaborate form of plain style, employing tropes and schemata, was popular with Richard Greenham, Arthur Dent, Archbishop Sandys, Bishop Jewel, Edmund Grindal, and Robert Humston, Bishop of Down and Conner.[69]

The colloquial style, which, according to Blench, "uses a racy and pungent speech idiom and avoids the schemata, but is enriched by frequent homely *exempla*," was skillfully used in the pre-Reformation period by Roger Edgeworth in his parish at Bristol, and, later, among the early reformers, notably Hugh Latimer, whose racy language is characterized thus: "What, ye brain-sick fools, ye hoddy-pecks, ye doddy-pouls, ye huddes, do ye believe him? are you

---

or metaphor, the 'narration' which is a story with human actors, and the 'fable' which is a story where the actors are animals."

[65]Ibid.

[66]Ibid., p. 168.

[67]Ibid.

[68]Ibid., pp. 170-73.

[69]Ibid., pp. 174-78.

seduced also?"[70] In the Edgeworth and Latimer tradition, John Bridges, Fellow of Pembroke College, Cambridge, and later Dean of Salisbury, and Henry Bedel, Vicar of Christ Church, London, are representatives of the colloquial style during the Elizabethan age.

The ornate style, which aims at oratorical display, employs both schemata and *exempla* on a wide scale to achieve the desired rhetorical effects. Among the pre-Reformation Catholics, Fisher and Longland are notable ornate preachers; among the Marians, James Brooks, Leonard Pollard, and Bishop Thomas Watson; among the Elizabethans, chiefly Richard Hooker.[71]

Blench places one other style in a separate category, regarding it as the bridge between the plain style and the fully ornate because it makes use of elements of both. He regards four Elizabethan preachers as representatives of this "richly coloured style": George Abbot, Ralph Tyrer, John King, and Henry Smith. Of Smith, he writes:

> There has been some controversy whether Henry Smith is a plain or an ornate preacher; G. P. Krapp finds him predominately plain, but A. F. Herr and Fritz Pützer see him as ornate. The truth surely lies between these extremes, for although his diction is simple, and often his use of the schemata is, as Herr says, 'stolid'; nevertheless his sermons are given rich and varied colour by very frequent masterly similes, which are often combined in a series, each member of which throws some illumination on the subject.[72]

Elizabethan preachers, therefore, could choose from a variety of styles the one best suited to their individual temperaments and needs; by its force, whether plain, colloquial, ornate, or somewhere between or in combination, they sought to fulfill the Augustinian aim of preaching: *docere, delectare et movere.* Even though no preacher followed a single form and style at all times, the thrust of his work

---

[70]Ibid., p. 142.

[71]Ibid., pp. 129-91.

[72]Ibid., p. 184.

usually permits him to be classified as plain, colloquial, or ornate in style, and ancient, New Reformed, or "modern" in his form.

Because of its bearing on Henry Smith, one aspect of Elizabethan worship that has to do with the participation of congregations might be profitably explored: the use of shorthand to record sermons. Of the few studies in existence on Henry Smith, one deals exclusively with the pirating of his sermons by the so-called "Characterie-takers," and Smith is by no means alone among the abused divines. Many Elizabethan churchgoers were serious worshipers and attentive listeners. Many were avid note-takers; and some, like John Manningham, have left valuable diaries filled with notes of sermons and lectures. Alan Fager Herr writes:

> When a sermon had been preached, there remained more than the preacher's notes from which to reconstruct it if it were decided that the sermon should be published. It was a common practice of members of the congregation to take notes, and a collation of these notes would furnish a fairly accurate copy of the *substance* of a sermon. It has been suggested [by W. F. Mitchell, *English Pulpit Oratory from Andrewes to Tillotson*, pp. 30ff.] that in the sixteenth century the practice of taking notes of sermons was an attempt to preserve a corpus of Protestant exegesis. In the seventeenth century the practice became more general, and note-taking was part of the school training of children. It is rather surprising to see how full and minute the notes of devout Elizabethans who transcribed their sermon notes into their diaries can be.[73]

Some of the note-takers were so accurate that they hardly missed a word. These notes were often amplified and published, often with remarkable fidelity. Some preachers were grateful to the note-takers who preserved their pulpit utterances. For example, Symon Presse, in the dedicatory remarks of "A Sermon Preached at Eggington" in 1596, thanks several of his parishioners for their diligence in preserving that sermon by notes and for spreading his name abroad among their friends and to the Lord Chief Justice of the Common Pleas:

---

[73]Herr, p. 77-78.

> To his loving parishioners Mr. F. Cooke, R. Johnson, W. Walton, R. Knight, J. Gyllyver, & R. Slygh increase of true zeale & endless felicitie. When I understood your attention in the hearing of this sermon, & diligence in noting certaine principall points, & paines in conferring together, penning, acquainting & sending your collections unto many your worshipfull friendes, & at the length unto the right honorable Sir Edmund Anderson knight, Lord Chief Justice of the Common Pleas, with intent (as I gesse) to make my simple skill liked and allowed of them, I thought it my duty to accept your endeavour very kindly, and to requite you with procuring the same sermon to be imprinted, that all men might give you deserved commendations, and note your names amongst the number of vigilant hearers to your immortal praise.[74]

Before 1588, when Timothy Bright published his work entitled *Characterie: An Arte of Shorte, Swifte, and Secrete Writing by Character*, sermon notes were taken in longhand. Thereafter, however, some churchgoers—presumably, like those referred to by Parson Presse—mastered so thoroughly this first system of shorthand that they were able to take down sermons *verbatim*. For-example, Anthony Tyrell, in the preface to "A Fruitfull Sermon," published in 1589, writes:

> The cause therefore why it [this sermon] is come forth, in brief, was this. At the time I made my exhortation publicklie in Christ his Church in London, my wordes were no soner out of my mouth but a young youth had penned my Sermon *verbatim* by Characterie, an art newly invented. It was this youthes pleasure, for the manifesting of his skill in that swift kind of writing, to publish my Sermon in print.[75]

Alan Herr points out that by 1593 sermons published from "Characterie" were so common that printers began advertising their sermons "as *not* having been written up from shorthand notes."[76] Indeed, not everyone who took shorthand had thoroughly mastered

[74]Ibid., p. 78.

[75]Ibid., p. 80.

[76]Ibid.

the art, and very often preachers were misquoted and, consequently, greatly angered by the "Characterie-takers." The author of a 1593 sermon entitled "Resurgendum" is quick to point out that the printed sermon is from "the Authors owne pen" and not patched together from any "new found Characterisme (which to the great prejudice of some worthie and learned, hath of late verie pitifully blemished some part of their [the preachers'] labours this way with intollerable mutilations)."[77]

The sermons of Henry Smith did not escape the "Characterie-takers," and his unbounded popularity as a preacher makes it easy for us to understand why.[78] In 1590, for example, Roger Ward printed Smith's sermon on "The Benefit of Contentation" for John Proctor. The sermon was advertised as "Taken by Characterie," and the following remarks are from its preface:

> To the Reader. There came to my hands (gentle Reader) the copie of a Sermon, which intreateth of couetousnes, which though it were not the authors minde or consent that it shoulde come foorth thus in market, yet considering that it is a doctrine so necessarie for these dayes, wherein it said, that Charities shall waxe colde, I thought good to commit it to the presse, preferring the profit and vtility of many in publishing it, before the pleasure of the Authour in concealing it.[79]

As Thompson Cooper points out, Smith took umbrage at the appearance of the pirated sermon and during the following year

---

[77]Ibid.

[78]Ibid., pp. 27-28: "The Elizabethans were NOT only pleased to listen to sermons, and those much longer than present day sermons, but they also read sermons in print for pleasure and edification. The sale of printed sermons was encouraging to the printers and as a result publications of sermons increased steadily throughout the reign. . . . Sometimes it was the preacher's name that sold the sermons. Henry Smith's sermons went into a phenomenal number of editions and his name on a sermon was so attractive to buyers that it was charged that unscrupulous printers forged sermons over his name when they could not lay their hands upon authentic copy."

[79]Thompson Cooper, "The Early Use of Shorthand," *Notes and Queries*, Eighth Series, 10 (5 September 1896), p. 189.

issued through Abell Jeffers's press his own corrected version of "The Benefit of Contentation."[80] In his preface, Smith addresses his readers thus:

> Hearinge how fast this Sermon hath vttered, & yet how miserablye it hath bin abused in Printing, as it were with whole lims cut off at once, and cleane left out, I haue taken a little paines (as my sicknesse gaue me leaue) both to perfit the matter, and to correct the print. Now as the Angell saide to John, Take this Booke & eate it: So I wish that thou hadste so digested this doctrine, that all the parts of thy body and soule were strengthened by it. But if al this will not make thee content with that thou hast, sorrow that thy Couetousnes is greater than others: and neuer loue thy selfe vntill thou can finde in thy hart to be blessed. Farewell. Thine H. Smith.[81]

Smith's unhappiness with the "Characterie-takers" did not, however, keep them from taking down his sermons. In fact, the demand for his printed sermons was so great that printers "employed shorthand writers to take down 'in characterie' many of his pulpit utterances."[82] His sermon entitled "The Wedding Garment" was apparently pirated, for in his own 1591 edition he referred to false

---

[80]Ibid.

[81]Ibid.

[82]Ibid. Cf. W. Fraser Mitchell, *English Pulpit Oratory from Andrewes to Tillotson* (London: Society for Promoting Christian Knowledge, 1932), 36-37: "Dr. Evelyn Simpson, in her discussion of one of Donne's sermons appearing in 'Sapientia Clamitans,' . . . has illustrated some of the possibilities of the case from different editions, authentic and 'pirated' of a sermon by Henry Smith, a Puritan lecturer of St. Clement Danes, whose preaching was in great estimation round about 1590. This preacher's popularity invited piracy, and we have in one instance a sermon printed from his manuscript and a 'pirated' version of the same, which is openly described as a sermon 'taken by Characterie,' and 'published for the benefit of the faithful.' Smith's printed sermons supply us also with an instance of a sermon 'taken by Characterie,' and published (apparently without the preacher's consent), the same sermon 'taken by Characterie and examined after' (presumably by the preacher), and the further version of the same, 'newly examined and corrected by the author.' This goes to show that the printing of sermons from notes taken by auditors might be of two sorts, either deliberate connivance, or even with the consent of the preacher. Where sermons

copies "printed without his knowledge, patched, as it seemed, out of some borrowed notes."[83] Further, as Thompson Cooper writes, "there were two editions printed in 1591 of 'The Restitution of King Nebuchadnezzar,' and in Smith's collected sermons is an address to the reader, stating that this and two other sermons on Nebuchadnezzar had been printed earlier from an imperfect copy, 'having in some places the minde of the Authour obscured, in other some the sentences unskillfully patched together.' "[84] These were not the only ones of Smith's sermons to be pirated, nor were he and other popular preachers the sole victims of the "Characterie-takers." Their skills were unquestionably employed in obtaining pirated plays and other public works for which printers felt a demand.[85]

However, even though Henry Smith was incensed at the pirated editions of his sermons which appeared in bookstalls all over England, their very appearance there attested to his great popularity. An early observer, William Burton, writes of Smith as that "learned and eloquent Divine whose excellent Sermons so often printed, doe publish sufficiently his fame and worthinesse to the world."[86]

---

were delivered *extempore* it is obvious that considerable variation might exist between the sermon as written up and published from the preacher's notes and the sermon as published from the notes of a stenographist."

[83]Ibid.

[84]Ibid., pp. 189-90.

[85]Cf. Matthias Levy's treatise, *Shakespeare and Shorthand* (London: J. Wade, 1884).

[86]William Burton, *The Description of Leicester Shire, Containing Matters of Antiquitye, Historye, Armorye, and Genealogy* (London: Printed for John White, 1622), p. 313.

CHAPTER 3

The Sermons of Henry Smith

SO POPULAR were the sermons of Henry Smith that they won for him not only the respect and admiration of his congregation at St. Clement Danes, the patronage of the powerful Lord Burghley, and the applause of Thomas Nashe, but also a loyal and extensive reading public. By 1610 Smith's printed sermons had gone through eighty-five or more editions and his fame as a powerful preacher survived him for several decades.

In order to appreciate Smith fully today, one must be familiar with some of the reasons for his great popularity during the reign of Queen Elizabeth. Before examining the sermons themselves, however, a word needs to be said about the text which has been used and a few of the bibliographical problems associated with the arrangement of the sermons. Thereafter, our attention may be profitably focused on his subject matter, especially topics of special interest, sermon form and style, and the harmony of matter and manner.

The text used in this study is the two-volume edition of the collected works published in 1866 in Nichol's Series of Standard Divines under the general editorship of Thomas Smith. These two volumes contain the known works of Henry Smith: (1) fifty-six sermons with six prefaces to the readers; (2) Smith's declaration to the Lord Justices regarding the visionary, Robert Dickons, and some unanswered questions gathered by Smith out of Dickons's confession; (3) Smith's long treatise in six chapters entitled *God's Arrow against Atheism and Irreligion* and John Danter's dedicatory epistle of that treatise to Lady Katherine Hayward; (4) eight prayers; (5) "A Comfortable Speech, taken from a Godly Preacher lying upon his Deathbed; Written for the Sick"; (6) "A Letter to One's Friend in his Sickness"; (7) eight epigrams; (8) *Micro-cosmo-graphia: The Little World's Description,* from Latin sapphics of Henry Smith, translated by Joshua Sylvester and dedicated to the Right Honourable Honoria Lady Hay; and (9) *The Life of Mr. Henry Smith* in three and one-third pages by Thomas Fuller, to which the general editor of the 1866 edition affixes eleven pages of notes.

The text of Thomas Smith's 1866 collected edition is based on that of Thomas Fuller's 1675 edition.[1] According to Thomas Smith, his 1866 edition "contains all the prose works of Smith that there is any reason to suppose ever to have existed, and Sylvester's translation of one of his Latin poems and of several of his epigrams."[2] Whenever Smith finds the 1675 text to be in error, he corrects it by referring to earlier editions in which "in almost every such case," he writes, "we have found a manifestly better reading."[3] In brief, Thomas Smith writes thus of his edition of Henry Smith's sermons:

> Upon the whole, we trust that this edition, as it is unquestionably the fullest, the most accurate, and the most elegant hitherto published, will be found to do fair justice to the author's fame.[4]

According to the general editor, the text of the 1866 edition is "the most accurate . . . hitherto published." Proof of that assertion lies

---

[1]Cf. Thomas Smith, ed., *The Works of Henry Smith,* 2 vols. (Edinburgh: James Nichol, 1866), 1:xx, where Smith states that his text is "that of the edition of 1575." The 1575 date is in error and should read 1675. Subsequent quotations from this edition are cited by volume and page number in the text.

[2]Ibid.

[3]Ibid., p. xxi.

[4]Ibid.

beyond the domain of this study; for, as Thomas King Ehret writes in his *Four Sermons of Henry Smith: A Critical Edition,* "the bibliographical problems associated with Smith's work are of a most complicated nature and would require a large-scale bibliographical study embracing the whole of his work before any definitive conclusions could reasonably be offered."[5] Spot checks of the 1866 text have been made against Thomas Ehret's 1968 edition of four of the sermons, and the 1866 text appears to be substantially in accord with Ehret's version; variations are minor and do not alter the meaning. Certainly, for the purposes of the present study, the 1866 edition is adequate. It is also the latest and unquestionably the most accessible, complete edition.

The principal textual problems surrounding Smith's sermons derive from the great number of published editions. His first sermon was published in 1589; by 1610 more than eighty-five editions had appeared in print, either singularly or in collections. Thomas Smith writes:

> The early editions of separate sermons were exceedingly numerous. Some of them were printed surreptitiously from shorthand notes, and he [Henry Smith] was obliged to publish them in self-defence. The copyright of these different publications being in different hands, it was of course difficult to get a collected edition of his works. This was accomplished in 1657, when Thomas Fuller stated in his preface, "That this useful and desired volume of sermons, &c., have been for some years past in a manner smothered, to the regret of many, is not to be imputed as the fault of any one man, it being occasioned by the diversity of interests to the said copies of sermons, treatises, &c." This edition of Fuller's is of a somewhat composite character. . . . This is an exceedingly neat volume. It was reprinted in 1575 [*sic,* i.e., 1675], but in inferior style, and with very numerous typographical errors. It is a copy of this edition that our printers have had in their hands, but we have corrected an immense number of blunders by collation with older editions, the

[5]Thomas King Ehret, *Four Sermons of Henry Smith: A Critical Edition* (dissertation, University of Illinois, Urbana IL, 1968), p. xcii.

> best in our possession, so far as it goes, being that of 1599. (1:xvii-xviii)

As Thomas Smith points out, Henry Smith published a number of his sermons himself in order to correct those which were surreptitiously and inaccurately printed. Evidence clearly suggests that Smith was concerned about textual problems and strove for textual reliability and that he was offended at the corruption of his text in a number of pirated sermons. In revising "The Benefit of Contentation" for the press, Smith notes that he had taken "paines (as my sicknesse gaue me leaue) both to perfit the matter, and to correct the print."[6] Also in the interest of textual reliability, Smith felt compelled, as Ehret notes, to revise "The Wedding Garment"

> in order to controll those false copies of this sermon, which were printed without my knowledge, patched (as it seemeth) out of some borrowed noates: and to stop the Printing of it againe without my corrections.[7]

Like the question of textual reliability, the order, or arrangement, of the sermons poses another complex bibliographical problem. If, indeed, Smith died in 1591, as Thompson Cooper and others suggest, he is cleared of the imputation of carelessness in the arrangement of the collected sermons, for the first edition would not have appeared until a year after his death; hence, any fault in the arrangement of the sermons must rest upon the editors. However, even the 1866 edition, which claims to be of all editions "unquestionably the fullest, the most accurate, and the most elegant hitherto published,"[8] fails to offer a reliable chronological arrangement of sermons.

---

[6]Thompson Cooper, "The Early Use of Shorthand," *Notes and Queries*, 8th Series, 10 (5 September 1896), p. 189. Cf. Thomas King Ehret, *Four Sermons of Henry Smith*, pp. lxxix-xcii, for a discussion of nineteen of the collected editions of Smith's sermons, beginning with the 1592 edition and ending with the edition of 1866.

[7]Thomas King Ehret, *Four Sermons of Henry Smith*, p. lxxviii.

[8]Thomas Smith, ed., *The Works of Henry Smith*, 1:xxi.

Thomas King Ehret, in his critical edition of four of Smith's sermons, attempts to place some of them in chronological order. He outlines his procedure as follows:

> I have approached the problem in four ways. First, the examination of internal evidence (references to the Armada, comments such as "I could not choose a fitter scripture than this which I handled last, which speakes of the renuing of our mindes") proved helpful in grouping some of the sermons. Second, some of the sermons were obviously preached in a sequence (two on the Last Supper; four on Jonah; three on Nebuchadnezzar). Third (and purely theoretical), Smith often uses scriptural passages for his text which are also assigned readings in the *Prayer Book*. It seems highly plausible that Smith would want to expound to his hearers the reading lesson for the day. Fourth, *The Stationers' Register* furnished helpful clues on terminal dating.[9]

For most of Smith's sermons, however, clues regarding arrangement do not exist; furthermore, as Ehret observes, "it is difficult to discover a stylistic development which might help date a sermon as early or late."[10] Hence, few of the sermons can be specifically dated; conjectures, however, are possible.

Ehret is quite correct in placing Smith's sermon "The Lost Sheep Is Found" at the beginning of his career, and he does so for the right reason, too, namely because the sermon "deals with his [Smith's] examination of Robert Dickons,"[11] the visionary who thought himself to be "Elijah, sent from God to perfect some defects in the prophecy of Malachi."[12] Noting that the sermon does not appear in any known edition before 1607, Ehret dates the sermon 1597 on the basis of John Nichols's statement that "Mr. Henry

---

[9]Thomas King Ehret, *Four Sermons of Henry Smith,* pp. xvii-xviii.

[10]Ibid., p. xxii.

[11]Ibid., p. xviii.

[12]Thomas Fuller, *The Church History of Britain; from The Birth of Jesus Christ until the Year M.DC.XLVIII,* ed. J. S. Brewer (Oxford: Oxford University Press, 1845), 5:7-8.

Smith was living in 1597; for in that year, he published, 'The Lost Sheep Is Found.' "[13] A more likely date, however, is 1582; for, according to Bishop Thomas Fuller, in *The Church History of Britain*, "This year [A.D. 1582] Robert Dickons . . . by God's blessing on the endeavors of Mr. Henry Smith, (whom his uncle, Mr. Briant Cave, this year sheriff of Leicestershire, employed therein) . . . was reclaimed, renouncing his blasphemies by subscription under his own hand."[14]

The two sermons on "The Art of Hearing" are also dated 1587 by Ehret, primarily on the basis of Smith's remarking in the first sermon, "methought I should go no further until I had taught you *how to hear.*"[15] It is impossible to ascertain the year in which these sermons were preached, but certainly one followed the other; the text of both is Luke 8:18 ("Take heed how you hear"). These two sermons are followed, in turn, by "The Heavenly Thrift," based also on Luke 8:18. The latter sermon begins, "The next words before are, 'Take heed how you hear' "; the reason follows (1:341).

A number of Smith's sermons can be arranged in groups, even though specific dates cannot be assigned to them. "The Sinner's Conversion" and "The Sinner's Confession" are companion sermons, based again on Luke, Smith's favorite gospel. Both sermons deal with Zaccheus, the publican who received Christ. These two sermons are followed by "The Betraying of Christ," which is an obvious sequel to the two sermons on Zaccheus; for it begins, "The last time you heard how a publican received Christ; now you shall hear how an apostle betrayed Christ" (1:409). Three other sermons

---

[13]John Nichols, *The History and Antiquities of the County of Leicester* (London, 1795), 2:2:889. It should be noted that Nichols contradicts himself on the point of Smith's death, for in the same *History* (2:2:468) he records the entry of Smith's death in the parish register of Husbands Bosworth: "Anno 1591, Henricus Smyth, theologus, filius Erasmi Smyth, armigeri, sepult. fuit 4to die Julii."

[14]Thomas Fuller, *The Church History of Britain*, 5:7-8.

[15]Thomas Smith, ed., *The Works of Henry Smith*, 1:320.

in a series, also based on Luke, are "The Lawyer's Question" (Luke 10:25), "The Lawgiver's Answer to the Lawyer's Question" (Luke 10:26), and "The Censure of Christ upon the Lawyer's Answer" (Luke 10:28). Two sermons on Genesis 9 are companion sermons, "Noah's Drunkenness" and "A Glass for Drunkards." Complementary sermons on the Last Supper are based on 1 Corinthians 11; complementary sermons on usury are based on Psalms 15:1-5. Another of Smith's favorite texts is Romans. "The Humility of Paul" and "A Looking-Glass for Christians" are based on Romans 12; "The Wedding Garment" and "The Way to Walk In," on Romans 13.

Internal evidence allows "The Sinful Man's Search" to be dated as a New Year's sermon. In it Smith says: "Let us make it a day of newness of life, as it is the first day of the new year . . . ; work this reformation in thyself betimes, even to-day, even this first day of the new year" (2:340). Ehret dates the sermon 1 January 1588 because the sermon "is entered on the *Stationers' Register* for 26 December 1588."[16] Internal evidence reveals one other New Year's sermon in the Smith canon, namely, "The Godly Man's Request." In it Smith says:

> So many years as are past, so many years we are nearer to the last; and though the old year be gone, and a new year come, yet whether another shall come after this, as this came after the former, no man, I think, hath any promise of him that made time; for even these two days since the old year went out, many have gone the way which we all shall follow. (1:275-76)

Of this sermon Ehret writes, "I assume the year was 1589 since I believe Smith retired from the pulpit that year because of ill health."[17]

On a number of occasions, Smith refers directly or obliquely to the Spanish Armada, and these references are helpful in ordering

---

[16]Thomas King Ehret, *Four Sermons of Henry Smith*, p. xviii.

[17]Ibid., p. 35.

the sermons. For example, in "Satan's Compassing the Earth," Smith says:

> It is some vantage unto us to hear that the Spaniards are coming, before they come; and what number they have, and how they are appointed, that we may levy our forces accordingly. (2:17)

Since the Spanish Armada threat lasted from 21 July through 29 July 1588, "we know," writes Ehret, "this sermon was preached some time before July 21, 1588. Queen Elizabeth's *Prayer Book* assigns chapter 1 in Job for a morning lesson in June. I conjecture that the sermon was preached in June 1588."[18] The biblical text of "Satan's Compassing the Earth" is Job 1:7-8: "Then the Lord saith unto Satan, Whence comest thou? And Satan answered the Lord, saying, From compassing the earth." The first sentence of "Satan's Compassing the Earth" clearly indicates that another sermon on Job 1:7-8 preceded it. Smith begins: "I have spoken of the question already, now of the answer" (2:17). The question is the Lord's to Satan, "Whence comest thou?" That sermon is lost.

"The Trial of the Righteous," like "Satan's Compassing the Earth," contains what is generally regarded as a reference to the Spanish threat. If, indeed, Smith's ending of the sermon—"To which pleasures the Lord Jesus bring us, when this cloud of troubles is blown over us!"—is a reference to the Spanish threat of war, the sermon was preached sometime between 21 July and 29 July 1588.

"The Dialogue between Paul and King Agrippa" contains a reference to the Armada that indicates the sermon was preached after the defeat of the Spaniards on 29 July 1588:

> . . . as some giddy spirits think now, that they which are zealouser than themselves know not what they say or do, and impute all the troubles of the realm, and the invasion of the Spaniards, unto the preaching of the word, and to the fasts and prayers that were exercised about that time. (1:436)

---

[18]Ibid., p. 2. Cf. p. xix.

Ehret places the sermon in August 1588 on the grounds that its biblical text is assigned for that month by the Prayer Book.[19]

"The Ladder of Peace" also refers to the defeat of the Spaniards:

> One would think that our deliverance out of Egypt, that our victory against the Spaniards, that the weather which threateneth sickness, that the dearth which threateneth famine, should make us pray, and yet doth not. (1:402)

Obviously, "The Ladder of Peace" was preached after 29 July 1588.[20] The biblical text of "The Ladder" is 1 Thessalonians 5:16-18: "Rejoice evermore. Pray continually. In all things give thanks." The first sentence of the "The Ladder" refers to a lost sermon on the same text: "When I spake last of these words, I shewed you how the apostle commendeth unto us three virtues." Another sermon, "The True Trial of the Spirits," is evidently closely related to this series, for its text is 1 Thessalonians 5:19-22, and Smith begins the sermon by saying, "At the last time when I spake of these words, 'In all things give thanks,' and 'Quench not the Spirit.' " One or more sermons are missing, however, from the series, but all of them appear to be dated shortly after England's defeat of the Spaniards.

Three other sermons can with some reasonableness be dated close to the Armada incident, namely, the series of sermons on Nebuchadnezzar; for, in the first of the series, Smith says:

> So we think, if God would send a famine upon this land, that would make us fear him; but God hath sent a famine, and yet we do not fear him. If God would send an earthquake upon this land, that would make us fear him; but God hath sent an earthquake, and yet we do not fear him. If God would send a pestilence upon this land, that would make us fear him; but God hath sent a pestilence, and yet we do not fear him. If God would send war upon this land, that

---

[19]Ibid., pp. xx-xxi.

[20]Ibid., p. xx: "*The Ladder of Peace* may have been preached in later July . . . ; the *Prayer Book* assigns the text for this sermon sometime in July."

> would make us fear him; but God hath sent war, and yet we do not fear him. (1:176-77)

Although not strictly in this series, "A Dissuasion from Pride, and an Exhortation to Humility" refers to Nebuchadnezzar and is a further statement on the theme of pride which Smith had substantially developed in the Nebuchadnezzar series. It is likely that all four were preached shortly after the Spanish Armada attacked.

Smith preached four sermons on Jonah. Internal evidence in the first sermon of the series indicates that the two sermons on "The Sweet Song of Old Father Simeon" preceded the Jonah series, for in "The Calling of Jonah," Smith begins: "You have heard the sweet song of old father Simeon" (2:205). The third sermon in the Jonah series indicates that the whole series was preached sometime after July 1588, for Smith says:

> As surely as Jonah thought to arrive at Tarshish, so surely the Spaniards thought to arrive in England; but as Jonah's company wondered at this tempest, so at these Spaniards' destruction their fellows at home wondered, yea, were astonished, how their invincible power could be destroyed. (2:235)

Ehret conjectures that the series was preached in September since the Prayer Book "lists Jonah 4 for that month."[21]

"The Christian's Sacrifice," which purports to be the sum of "all the lessons together which ye have heard since I came [to St. Clement Danes]" (1:112), has a preface dedicated "To my late Auditors, the Congregation of Clement Danes" (1:111). The preface is signed "Your late unworthy servant for the Lord, H.S." (1:111). It is obvious that *late* does not denote "deceased"; it means "late of that parish," that is, that Smith has retired from the pulpit of St. Clement but is still alive. Then Smith writes, "ye have heard it already" (1:111). Hence, it is clear that Smith had preached "The Christian's Sacrifice" to his St. Clement congregation before his retirement and that now he has prepared it for the press.

---

[21]Ibid., p. xx.

"The Christian's Sacrifice" ends thus: "What shall I wish you now before my departure? . . . I have but one day more to teach you all that you must learn of me" (1:124-25). Clearly, "The Christian's Sacrifice" can be placed near the end of Smith's sermons. He has but one more day to preach at St. Clement Danes, and this sermon immediately precedes his final sermon. Ehret writes:

> There is an entry for "The Christian's Sacrifice" in the *Stationers Register* for 3 October 1589. This leads me to conclude that Smith retired from the pulpit sometime before this date. Proverbs 23, the text of this sermon, would have been read according to the *Prayer Book* sometime in July.[22]

"The Petition of Moses to God," according to a sentence in brackets at the end of it, "was the last sermon that Henry Smith made at St. Clement Danes" (1:431). At the beginning of the sermon, we have no indication that it is Smith's last. Throughout, it offers nothing striking to set it apart from the rest; in fact, it lacks the intensity of most of his sermons. The first indication that it is Smith's final utterance at St. Clement Danes comes in the next to the last paragraph where he says:

> Now it resteth that I should encourage Joshua, which succedeth me. But how shall I begin to encourage him? or where should I begin? Shall I tell him that he shall live now at ease and in security? No. How shall I encourage Joshua? Shall I tell him you will love him, and follow him, and that he shall find you willing and forward in every good action? If I promise it, shall I not lie? If I become bounden for you, shall I not forfeit? I fear yes. Why, how then should I encourage Joshua? Shall I tell him all will speak well of him? or shall I tell him none will slander him? No. For if he be as righteous as Christ, yet some of the scribes and pharisees will seek to persecute him. If he will live in quietness, he must not utter all the counsel of God, though God command him. Nor must he reprove some sins, for then he shall be thought to bear envy against some persons. Nor must he keep company among the godly, for then he shall be accounted a partaker. Nor must he deny the company of the wicked, for then he shall be accounted a precisian, a

[22]Ibid., p. xix.

> puritan, and I know not what. But thou wilt say, What then? I answer, Yes; and that is, it may be after some three or four years' labour and travail he shall win some two or three unto Christ, which shall extinguish all grief; for God will one day reward him for his labour, and glorify him in heaven. But if Joshua should be in trouble, as he cannot almost otherwise choose, if he keep a good conscience, and reprove the mighty under his charge, then he shall see most of the great ones will quite forsake him, which now seem to favour him; and they will see him persecuted like Christ, and stand afar off like Pilate, and wash their hands, as though they were innocent, when it is in their power and authority to amend it. (1:430-31).

For a farewell sermon, these are strong words; the language not only has a sting to it but sounds highly personal. The advice he offers his successor might well have been the advice he offered his congregation and, no doubt, himself in "The Trial of the Righteous": "Seeing then your kingdom is not here, look not for a golden life in an iron world" (1:247). Smith concludes his farewell sermon with an admonition to his congregation regarding their new preacher:

> Love him and obey him in all righteousness, as the Jews did their Joshua; and here I deliver you unto him, and with my love, leave, and good will, I give him my possessions, my labour, and my twelve months' travails. And here, because I would not keep you over long . . . , I will make an end, beseeching you, as Joshua besought the people of Israel, that you will henceforward fear the Lord, and serve him in truth. . . . (1:431)[23]

Smith preached at least once at Paul's Cross, but it is not known whether he preached there before or after his retirement from Clement Danes. Millar Maclure, in *The Paul's Cross Sermons,*

---

[23]When Smith says, "I would not keep your over long," he is expressing in words what appears to be always a concern—namely, that his sermons be kept within the bounds of reasonable limits (for that age at least). Most of his sermons are about the same length and would require about an hour to read aloud. Cf. "Jacob's Ladder; or, the Way to Heaven," where he writes, "Because I have but one hour to teach you all that you must learn of me, I have chosen a text which is like Jacob's ladder, that shews you the way to heaven" (2:81).

indicates that Smith delivered "The Trumpet of the Soul Sounding to Judgment" there *ante* 1593. The sermon itself also indicates that it was delivered from that popular pulpit. Smith says:

> When I should have preached under the cross, I mused what text to take in hand, to please all, and to keep myself out of danger; and musing, I could not find any text in the Scripture that did not reprove sin. (2:323)

Although Smith belongs to that group of moderate preachers who regarded themselves not as Puritans at all but as Anglicans, he is in many ways the embodiment of Puritanism in its deepest sense. Certainly the Puritan elements of his work are now its most interesting and vital aspects. A general survey of his subject matter reveals the Puritan thrust of Smith's mind.

First, like Chaucer's Aegeus, Smith regards the world as a thoroughfare of woe, as a testing-place to purify the soul for the world to come. In "The Sinful Man's Search," he writes:

> God hath placed us here in this world as husbandmen, to plough upon the fallow of our hearts; as labourers to work in the vineyard, as travellers to seek a country, as soldiers to fight the battle of the Lord, against the flesh, the world, and the devil. (2:335)

In "The Humility of Paul," Smith enumerates some of the ways of the world that must be avoided:

> Therefore "fashion not yourselves unto the world," lest you be in the devil's fashion. Then you must not prank up yourselves like players, for this is the fashion of the world; then you must not respect persons more than justice, for this is the fashion of the world; then you must not flatter to please, for this is the fashion of the world; then you must not deceive to grow rich, for this is the fashion of the world; then you must not seek revenge for every word, for this is the fashion of the world; then you must not take scorn to be told of your faults, for this is the fashion of the world; then you must not give alms to be seen, for this is the fashion of the world; then you must not obey for fear of the law, for this is the fashion of the world; then you must not receive the sacrament for order, for this is the fashion of the world; then you must not come to church for custom, for this is the fashion of the world; then you must not make religion but a table-talk, for this is the fashion of the

> world; then you must not turn with the time, for this is the fashion of the world; then you must not defer to do good till you die, for this is the fashion of the world. (1:463)[24]

To the true Christian, writes Smith, this world is so distasteful that death is to be longed for. His clearest expression of this theme is found in "The Sweet Song of Old Father Simeon":

> The fish [that] is taken in the net out of the sea struggleth to get in again; and Adam, thrust out of paradise, would fain have been within again: how much more should we be desirous to be settled in the new paradise, in assurance never to be put from thence? Therefore also it is not only our duty to desire death, but also as soon as any clearly seeth Christ, presently he desireth to die. For though his state be never so pleasant, though his life be most delightful, though he excel in riches, and pleasures, and honours, and knowledge, and glory, and far exceed all that ever were; yet at the sight of Christ he even rejoiceth to forego all; the love of the world falling away like the Mantle of Elias, when he was rapt into heaven; and so crieth with the apostle, "I desire to be dissolved," that he may be with Christ. (2:168)

The principal thrust of Smith's message, repeated again and again in the sermons, is derived from his view of the world as a place of vanity and sorrow. The Christian pilgrim, bound for the heavenly city, must always fight against the devices of the world, the lure of the flesh, the wiles of the devil. If he is to be successful in the struggle, he must put on the whole armor of God. Smith devotes an entire sermon to that garment which he calls "The Wedding Garment." His text is Romans 13:14, "Put ye on the Lord Jesus Christ." He begins the sermon, "I have chosen a text which is the

---

[24]Cf. "The Trumpet of the Soul Sounding to Judgment" (2:328) for an additional catalogue of sins, among them the following: "Item, for lending to usury; item, for racking of rents; item, for deceiving thy brethren; item, for falsehood in wares; item, for starching thy ruffs; item, for curling thy hair; item, for painting thy face; item, for selling of benefices; item, for starving of souls; item, for playing at cards; item, for sleeping in the church; item, for profaning the Sabbath day . . . ; the fornicator for taking of filthy pleasure . . . ; the careless prelate, for murdering so many thousand souls."

sum of the Bible" (1:147). Repeatedly, Smith urges his congregation to put on the Lord Jesus Christ, for Christ is man's only hope. In "The Sweet Song of Old Father Simeon," Smith writes:

> Christ is the fountain of all wisdom, of all righteousness, of all truth, of all knowledge, of all salvation, and briefly of all goodness; for there is no other ark to save us from the flood, no other ladder to ascend with into heaven, no other Joseph to feed us in the famine, no other Moses to lead us through the wilderness. (2:181)

In fact, Smith ends his career as a preacher by stating again this vital message: "Put ye on the Lord Jesus Christ." Having, as he says, "but one day more to teach you all that you must learn of me" (1:125), Smith aims at nothing short of "bind[ing] all the lessons together which ye have learned since I came" (1:112). As that message is "the sum of the Bible" in "The Wedding Garment," it is here "the sum of all my sermons" (1:111). Smith pleads:

> What shall I wish you now before my departure? I wish you would give all your hearts to God while I speak, that ye might have a kingdom for them. Send for your hearts where they are wandering, one from the bank, another from the tavern, another from the shop, another from the theatres; call them home, and given them all to God, and see how he will welcome them, as the father embraceth the son. (1:124)

A general survey of Smith's sermons indicates that many of his themes were the common concerns of the English church. All of the preachers warned against the snares of the world and urged their congregations to put on the armor of Christ; none, however, preached more intensely upon these themes than Smith. Like his fellow clergymen, Smith labored against the deadly sins. Pride is the subject of three sermons on Nebuchadnezzar, as well as "The Trial of Vanity" and a sermon entitled "A Dissuasion from Pride, and an Exhortation to Humility." Avarice is dealt with at length in two sermons on usury and in "The Benefit of Contentation." Envy is a central theme of "The Way to Walk In." Gluttony and immoderation in all its forms are excoriated in "Noah's Drunkenness" and "A Glass for Drunkards," and lechery is condemned, as continence is exalted in "A Preparative to Marriage." Also like his fellows, Smith extols the great virtues. Patience is praised in "The Trial of the Righteous"; love is contrasted with envy in "The Way to Walk In"; humility is the positive force that conquers pride in "A Dissuasion from Pride"; wisdom is that great good for which the godly man is urged to pray in "The Godly Man's Request"; obedience is the Christian virtue applauded in the four sermons on Jonah.

In addition to standard themes, Smith's sermons deal with others which, taken together, distinguish his sermons from those of his contemporaries. He regards himself as a competent spokesman on a wide spectrum of topics, ranging from the nursing of babies to the general state of preaching in England. Although a bachelor himself, he is quite emphatic in his opinion that mothers should breastfeed their babies. In "A Preparative to Marriage," he draws on a number of biblical examples to support his view:

> The first duty is the mother's, that is, to nurse her child at her own breasts, as Sarah did Isaac, Gen. xxi.7; and therefore Isaiah joineth the nurse's name and the mother's name both in one, and calleth them "nursing mothers;" shewing that mothers should be the nurses. So when God chose a nurse for Moses, Exodus ii.8, he led the handmaid of Pharaoh's daughter to his mother, as though God would have none nurse him but his mother. After, when the Son of God was born, his Father thought none fit to be his nurse but the virgin his mother, Mat. ii.14. The earth's fountains are made to give water, and the breasts of women are made to give suck. Every beast and every fowl is bred of the same that did bear it, only women love to be mothers, but not nurses. Therefore, if their children prove unnatural, they may say, Thou followest thy mother, for she was unnatural first, in locking up her breasts from thee, and committing thee forth like a cuckoo, to be hatched in a sparrow's nest. Hereof it comes that we say "He sucked evil from the dug;" that is, as the nurse is affected in her body or in her mind, commonly the child draweth the like infirmity from her, as the eggs of a hen are altered under the hawk. Yet they which have no milk, can give no milk. But whose breasts have this perpetual drought? Forsooth, it is like the gout; no beggars may have it, but citizens or gentlewomen. In the ninth chapter of Hosea, dry breasts are named for a curse; what lamentable hap have gentlewomen to light upon this curse more

> than others? Sure if their breasts be dry, as they say, they should fast and pray together, that this curse might be removed from them. (1:35-36)

Bishop Fuller records the impact of Smith's sermon on his congregation at Clement Danes:

> It is almost incredible how many persons of honour and worship, ladies and great gentlewomen, with whom his congregation was constantly crowded, were affected herewith, so that I have been informed, from such whose credit I count it a sin to suspect, that they presently remanded their children from the vicinage round about London, and endeavoured to discharge the second moiety of a mother, and to nurse them whom they had brought into the world. I confess some conceived Mr. Smith, because a bachelor, an incompetent judge hereof, as unacquainted with feminine infirmities, so that, as St. Augustine on another account was called *durus pater infantum*, so Mr. Smith might be termed *durus doctor matrum*. However, if all things be impartially considered, no just cause of exception can be found either with the doctrine or application. (1:ix)

Smith's sermons, however, generally reflect the broader concerns of the church, such as the dearth of ministers. During the reign of Elizabeth, many parishes were insufficiently staffed; some pulpits, altogether silent. Like all Puritans, Smith was particularly eager to rectify the problem. In "Mary's Choice," he writes:

> One thing is necessary, saith Christ; and what is that one thing? Even to hear the word preached, which is the power of God to salvation, to every one that believeth. A man may better want all things than that one needful thing. (2:361)

In "The Way to Heaven," Smith questions rhetorically:

> Are not pardons as good as works? are not pilgrimages as good as prayers? is not sacrifice as good as obedience? is not reading as good as preaching? May I not go to heaven this way and that way, as well as by the word? No; as no water but Jordan could cleanse Naaman's leprosy, so no way but the word can bring to heaven. (2:88)

In fact, the very words which the prophet Elisha used in sending for Naaman—Naaman "shall know that there is a prophet in Israel" (2 Kings 8)—suggest, as Smith writes in "The True Trial of the

Spirits," that "all the glory of Israel were chiefly in this, that they had prophets, and others had none; as if one parish should triumph over another, because they have a preacher, and the other have none" (2:134).

People should delight in their good fortune in having a preacher in the community to reveal to them God's plan of salvation, and their delight should be greater because of the unselfish character of the true physicians of the soul:

> Because they are like lamps, which consume themselves to give light to others, so they consume themselves to give light to you; because they are like a hen, which clucketh her chickens together from the kite, so they cluck you together from the serpent; because they are like the shout which did beat down the walls of Jericho . . . , so they beat down the walls of sin; because they are like the fiery pillar which went before the Israelites to the land of promise, so they go before you to the land of promise, because they are like good Andrew, which called his brother to see the Messias . . . , so they call upon you to see the Messias. (1:135)

Without a preacher, the spiritual life withers and dies; but too often, even with a preacher, people fail to have any real concern for their soul's need. In "Food for New-Born Babes," Smith laments:

> [T]his city, which should be the glory of the kingdom, may well be termed Golgotha, the place of dead men's skulls, in regard there are so many thousands souls dead in sin, dead in desire, who have no thirst and hunger for the word of God. If they have a bare reading minister, as children have a puppet to play with, they think themselves in a happy estate; as if Elisha's staff could raise the dead child without Elisha, and the word give life without a preacher. (1:490)

Thus, Smith emphasizes that it is incumbent upon the community to supply itself with a preacher, to search him out instead of waiting for him to seek them. He writes:

> I think you know my meaning. I would not wish you wait till preachers offer themselves to instruct you, but to send to the schools of learning, to provide godly and able men, who may minister the word in due season. (1:490)

Because heaven can be attained only by right living and because God's word is man's directive toward that end, the preacher is essential to the community. Smith writes: "Ye would rather desire your bodies might be without souls, than your churches without preachers" (1:495).

Furthermore, according to Smith, the true churchman has a responsibility not only to teach well but also to live well (2:129). Words and teaching alone are not enough. The quality of his life must support his words and be a witness of their truth. A preacher must be a whole man and a complete Christian example for others. Like Chaucer's parson, Smith knows that, if gold rusts, iron will rust much more; consequently, he is severe in his denunciation of preachers who fail to set a godly example themselves, believing that "they do more hurt by their bad example, than they can do good with all their preaching" (2:129). "Will not the people reason thus," writes Smith, "if his doctrine were good, surely he would follow it; if his life be good, surely he would teach us to live as he doth . . . ?" (2:128-29).

Some preachers, however, fail in their office because they are ill-prepared and do not fully know the duties of their calling or, worse still, because they have taken on the collar for worldly rather than spiritual reasons. In several sermons Smith writes against the ill-trained preacher and against the preacher who enters the Church uncalled. Of the latter, Smith writes in "The Calling of Jonah":

> None ought to take upon them the function of preaching in the church, unless they have their warrant or authority from God, as Aaron had, Heb. v.4. And although they have not their authority in that form and manner as Jonah had his, namely, as it were, by word of mouth even from God himself, 'Arise, and go to Nineveh,' yet they must have their warrant from him, else their calling is unlawful. (2:209)

Of the former type, the ill-trained preachers, Smith writes in "The True Trial of the Spirits":

> [N]one should meddle with the word (which is the law of God) but they which are fit, lest they make it despised. Hannah said, "I

> will not offer the child to God before he be weaned," 1 Samuel i.22, that is, before he be taken from the dug; but now they offer their children to God before they be weaned, before they can go, before they can speak; and send them to fight the Lord's battles before they have one stone in their hand to sling at Goliath, that is, one scripture to resist the tempter, Mat. iv. (1:139)

The ill-trained preacher and the uncalled preacher are more harmful to the Church than those who merely read a homily. These unequipped and self-appointed ministers are the Church's refuse, and Smith compares them to blasphemers, "for one takes the name of God in vain, and the other takes the word of God in vain" (1:336). "What a shame it is," laments Smith, "that preachers should make preaching so despised!" (1:337).

Such preachers are Satan's gift to the church, for Satan wants nothing so much as to destroy God's ministry on earth. Smith reminds his congregation of a few of Satan's methods in "The Affinity of the Faithful," where he relates how the devil tried to interrupt even the preaching of Christ by having his mother and relatives send for him. The devil, Smith points out, has many means to interrupt and thwart God's ministry:

> I shewed you Christ preaching, a great press hearing, his friends and kinsmen interrupting, and Christ again withstanding the interruption; by this you may see what a spite the devil hath to hinder one sermon; therefore no marvel though he cause so many to be put to silence; no marvel though he stand so against a learned ministry; no marvel though he raise up such slanders upon preachers; no marvel though he writes so many books against the Christian government in the church; no marvel though he make so many non-residents; no marvel though he ordain so many dumb priests; for these make him the god of this world; the devil is afraid that one sermon will convert us, and we are not moved with twenty; so the devil thinketh better of us than we are. (2:299)[25]

---

[25]Cf. Smith's first sermon on "The Art of Hearing" (1:320-21) where he elaborates further on the stumbling blocks which Satan casts in the way of preachers: "First, he labours all that he can to stay us from hearing [God's word]; to effect this, he keeps us at taverns, at plays, in our shops, and appoints us some

Despite the preacher's hard work, his efforts often come to nothing. Many are unable to speak with any real force, and most of the congregation are unable to hear with any real attention: "Such is the dumbness of preachers, and the deafness of all sorts of hearers," writes Smith, "that there is great slowness of followers, so that there is but little good done, and but a few fruits gathered" (2:212).

Few Preachers have the courage to reprove sin where they find it, and almost none in the congregation is able to take reproof in the right spirit; thus, what Smith calls "the necessariest office" is generally the most neglected, for "if a preacher reprove sin, he is thought to do it of hatred, or of some particular grudge, and to be too busy, too bitter, too sharp, too rough" (2:213). But the true servant of God is compelled to reprove, for how else can he cure men of their folly and guide them through sin's long labyrinth? Smith writes:

> [P]ersuade yourselves, beloved, which is most true, though we speak as if we were angry with you, and threaten as if we would hurt you, and cry against you as if we hated you, yet we love you in the dearest blood we have; and therefore, though with persecution we preach the law, to lead you to the gospel, we preach judgment that you may find mercy, we preach hell to bring you to heaven; whatsoever and howsoever we preach, we do all to fill your hearts with joy in believing, and, having made you fruitful in all good

---

other business at the same time, that when the bell calls us to the sermon, we say, like the churlish guests, We cannot come, Mat. xxii. If he cannot stay us away with any business or exercise, then he casts fancies into our minds, and drowsiness into our heads, and sounds into our ears, and sets temptations before our eyes; that though we hear, yet we should not mark. . . . If he cannot stay our ears, nor slack our attention as he would, then he tickleth us to mislike something which was said, and by that make us reject all the rest. If we cannot mislike anything which is said, then he infecteth us with some prejudice of the preacher; he doth not as he teacheth, and therefore we less regard what he saith . . . To compass this, so soon as we have heard, he takes us to dinner, or to company, or to pastime, to remove our minds, that we should think no more of it. If it stay in our thoughts . . . , then he hath this trick; instead of applying the doctrine, which we should follow, he turns us to praise and extol the preacher. He made an excellent sermon! he hath a notable gift! I never heard any like him!" (1:320-21).

> works, present you without spot, nay, glorious also, as a virgin most beautiful, to the Lord of all grace and glory, Christ Jesus. (2:231)

Glory and thanks are also due to him who turns others from sin to salvation, from death to life, from hell to heaven; but the glory of this world is not the preacher's reward, for the world will not glorify him who is not her own, him who wars against her. Inherent in the profession of preaching are those hardships which result from a full renunciation of the world, the flesh, and the devil. In his second sermon on "The Rebellion of Jonah," Smith reflects on his profession thus:

> [T]his is a stumbling vocation amongst men, yea, rejected by the children of this world, which always kick against it; so that if you would ask for a painful vocation, this is it; if for a thankless vocation, that is it; if for a contemptible vocation, this is it; for reproving, we are reproved; blessing, we are cursed; preaching peace, we make war; proclaiming liberty, we are imprisoned; do what we can, we are persecuted; and for our work worthy of love, we receive of the most hatred; of few, yea, very few, not any more than a cold affection. (1:230)

In such a manner the world rewards God's servants. The preacher who, if he received his just deserts, "is more to be honoured than the ruler," is despised instead (1:135). In "The True Trial of the Spirits," Smith writes:

> There be two trades in this land, without the which the realm cannot stand; the one is the king's soldiers, and the other is the Lord's soldiers; and the Lord's soldiers are handled like the king's soldiers; for, from the merchant to the porter, no calling is so despised, so contemned, so derided, that they may beg for their service, for their living is turned into an alms. One saith, that Moses is *quis*, that is, the magistrate is somebody; but Aaron is *quasi quis*, that is, the minister is nobody, because nobody is despised like him. . . . If Paul had lived in our days, he would not have said, "Despise not the prophets," but "Persecute not the prophets"; for he should have seen not only despisers of the prophets, but mockers of them: not only mockers of, but slanderers of them: not only slanderers, but hunters, and biters, and smiters of them. (1:136)

The true servant of God can be distinguished from the false, however, in one significant respect. The false prophet, who has sought the Church to find an easy life, is quickly discouraged when he finds only contempt where he thought to receive respect, and poverty where he looked for comfort and ease. He attempts to turn his misfortune into profit by neglecting his most important duties and becoming a pardoner of offences to win favor and a panderer of glib lies to secure preferments. Of this sort Smith writes:

> [T]he prophets neglect prophesying. The non-resident keeps himself away, because he thinks the people like him better because he doth not trouble them; and the drone never studieth to preach, for he saith that an homily is better liked of than a sermon; and they which would study divinity above all, when they look upon our contempt, and beggary, and vexation, turn to law, to physic, to trades, or anything, rather than they will enter this contemptible calling. (1:138)

Unlike the false prophets, the true servants of God refuse to prostitute themselves or their calling for personal gain, but suffer gladly the displeasure of men to win the approval of God. They consider themselves blessed when they suffer for God's sake. Smith writes in his first sermon on "The Art of Hearing" that, "as the lambs breed in winter, and quails come with the wind, so [true] preachers spring in the time of discouragement more than when nothing hindereth them" (1:319). With willing hearts, they preach the Gospel of Christ to a world they know is set against them; under the protecting armor of Jesus, they meet Satan and all his forces of evil and defeat them.

Because of the importance Henry Smith attached to preaching, he would not have entered the ministry himself had he not been certain such was God's will. Although his family pushed him toward the profession of law, he persisted in his desire to be a churchman. A passage in "The Affinity of the Faithful" sounds particularly autobiographical when Smith writes on the various voices which tempt one to forsake the ministry, voices like those of Christ's mother and kinsmen that call one from God's service:

> Many privileges, many offices, and many benefices, have stopped to this voice, Thy mother calleth thee, or, Thy kinsmen would have

> thee. As this voice came to Christ while he was labouring, so many such voices come to us while we are labouring. One saith, Pleasure would speak with you; another saith, Profit would speak with you; another saith, Ease would speak with you; another saith, A deanery would speak with you; another saith, A bishopric would speak with you; another saith, The court would speak with you. When a man is in a good way, and studies the Scriptures to be a teacher of the church, a voice cometh to his ear, as this came to Christ's and saith, Thy friends would have thee study the law, for by divinity thou shalt attain to no preferment, and thine own flock will vex thee, or a bishop will stop thy mouth. . . . If he be a divine already, and preach his conscience, a voice cometh unto him again, as this did to Christ, and saith, Thy friends would have thee to be quiet; or, There be spies which do note what thou sayest; or, There be fellows that lie in wait for thy living. . . . Thus we are cumbered like our Master, before our sermons, and in our sermons, and after our sermons; even of them sometime, which should encourage us; and therefore, as Christ saith, "Beware of men," Mat. x.17, so say I, Beware of kinsmen. (2:294)

Smith insists that, if one is to devote full service to God, one must forsake the voices of the world. When one takes on the hard liberty of the Church, he must forsake wealth, worldly positions, preferments of all kinds, devoting his talents to God's service by diligent study and prayer. Although preachers are obliged to perfect their knowledge by study, they are recipients also of one of heaven's special blessings—divine revelation. Divine revelation is God's gift, free, and not obtainable by study; it is God's reward to the pure heart, not to the commodious mind; it is God's voice, not man's; the preacher is but the means by whom God's will is made manifest to men.

In "The Christian's Practice," Smith writes, "As Adam's knowledge was perfect, so long as his righteousness was untainted; so the nearer we come to that righteousness again, the more things come to our knowledge" (1:255). Thus, when a man opens his heart to God, God enlightens his mind with understanding. Therefore, "holy and righteous men cannot give any reason why they conceive the words of God so easily, and the wicked do conceive them so hardly; but that God brings the meaning suddenly to their hearts" (1:254). When the preacher's own understanding is illumined by God's infinite wisdom, he becomes the means of God's divine revelations to men. He is at that moment no ordinary man; he is God's vessel; he is God's viceroy and, as such, his dignity and worth surpass that of other men. However foolish he may appear to be in the eyes of the world, his foolishness is, at the time of his illumination, turned to wisdom and deserves to be heeded. In "The True Trial of the Spirits," Smith elaborates on this idea:

> Some come to hear us as Naaman came to Elisha; when the prophet had told him what he should do, he mocked him for it; he thought that he knew a better way than that himself, 2 Kings v.11. So they come to hear us, but they think they can teach us; but they must remember that Paul saith, "God hath chosen the foolish to confound the wise," 1 Cor. i.27. Therefore, if they think themselves wise, let them think us those fools whom God hath chosen to confound them; for although at all other times we are plain and simple as Jacob, yet at this time we have a promise, and it is given to us for your sake to speak sometime that which we conceive not ourselves, because the hour is come wherein God hath appointed to call some of you, as he hath done some of you before. Therefore, as the princely spirit came upon Saul when he should reign, to teach him how he should rule, 1 Sam. xi.6, so the prophetical spirit cometh upon preachers when they should teach, to teach them how they should speak. Therefore, as Christ was contented to be baptized of John, Mat. iii.18, so be you contented to be instructed of us, that if we be more simple than you, the glory of God may appear more in converting you by us. (1:138)[26]

God reveals his divine wisdom through prophets and preachers for the benefit of all mankind. This revelation is not for the benefit of the prophet and indicates no superior wisdom which would set him apart from the rest of men; revelation has nothing to do with earthly wisdom, nor should the latter be exalted as the

---

[26]Cf. Smith's first sermon on "The Art of Hearing," (1:325), where he repeats verbatim these words, beginning ". . . although at all other times we are plain and simple."

source of the former. Revelation comes from God, and to God must go the praise. In his first sermon on "The Calling of Jonah," Smith writes:

> Daniel said, that the Lord did not reveal the king's dream unto him for any wisdom that he had more than any living, but only for the king's sake, and for the poor people of God's sake, Dan. ii.30. And so you must think of us that are the ministers of the gospel, that the Lord doth not reveal his will unto us for any wisdom or worthiness that is in us more than other men, but for your sakes, and that we might reveal it to you. Therefore hear us even for this cause, because the Lord hath revealed unto us these things for your sakes and good. (2:210)

Armed with the knowledge gleaned from his own diligent study and with God's gift of divine revelation, the true preacher is prepared to fight the Goliaths of the world; but victory cannot easily be achieved, however well armed the preacher is. The battle will be won only after the greatest struggle, and no available means of assistance can be neglected. The preacher has at his disposal two powerful weapons, zeal and discretion, which support him in his war against the world.

According to Smith, "zeal and discretion united together, are like the two lions which supported the throne of Solomon" (1:130); "as wine is tempered with water," writes Smith, "so let discretion temper zeal" (1:130). In his view, however, the English Church does not have enough zealous preachers to need tempering. The wine of their zeal is already diluted. Smith writes in "The True Trial of the Spirits":

> I need not bring water to quench that fire that is out already. I would rather I could say of you, You are too zealous, as Paul told the Athenians, they were too superstitious, Acts xvii.22. But our sickness is not a hot sickness, but a cold sickness; the hot body is distempered, but the cold body is dead. Zeal was never infamous before our days; the papists are commended if they be zealous; but the protestant, if he be zealous, is held in derision. (1:130-31)

Zealous preachers, however few, alarmed both the Queen and her government with their prophesying. Sects sprouted up all over

England, each with its own zealots and its own doctrine. In an effort to bring to order the ensuing confusion, the Queen herself issued an edict to prohibit prophesying. But to prohibit prophesying, according to Smith, is to quench the spirit. Paul wrote, "Quench not the Spirit," and he followed that admonition with another, "Despise not prophesying." Smith writes:

> [I]t is as if Paul should say, Quench not the Spirit by despising of prophesying; neither despise prophesying, because all do not prophesy alike; but rather, when you hear some preach one way, and some another, when you see some follow him, and others follow him, do you try the doctrines by the Scripture, as the men of Berea did, Acts xvii.11, and choose that which is best, and soundest, and truest, having always such an eye to the truth, that you abstain from all appearance of error. (1:132)

He also warned his congregation, as Paul warned the Thessalonians, that, "If any prophets among them do not as they teach, and therefore seem worthy to be despised, like the Scribes and Pharisees, yet that they take heed that they do not despise prophesying for the prophets" (1:133-34). Conversely, the danger abides—however remote it may be—that a congregation will love its preacher inordinately and thereby place him higher in their regard than his doctrine which goes untried against the Scriptures because of him from whom it proceeds. Smith's view is characteristic: "If we should make much of prophets, how much should we make of prophesying! If we should love our instructors, how much should we love instruction?" (1:135). Unfortunately, however, most Protestants, according to Smith, love neither the prophet nor his prophesying. Unlike the papists who commend those who are zealous in prophesying, Protestants lack enthusiasm. Among Protestants, "If there be any that be more forward in religion than the rest, and more diligent to hear the word, as Mary was, there shall not want some or other to censure them at their pleasure, yea, to find fault, and condemn them for so doing" (2:359).

The Queen and her government feared religious zeal, not because of its bearing on religious practice or religious thought, but because of its effect, when misdirected, on order in the kingdom. Yet most of the Puritan preachers, except the very radical, looked with favor on both the government and its Queen and preached sermons on the necessity of order and obedience. Henry Smith has a great deal to say about order, hierarchy, obedience, duty, and the like, as touching both kings and their subjects, parents and their children, masters and their servants. His thinking follows an established tradition and represents an attitude most congenial with, and in no way threatening to, the wishes of any Christian sovereign.

In "A Memento for Magistrates," for example, Smith preaches on the necessity of man's observing station, order, and degree. He proclaims that "every man is to be content with that estate wherein God hath placed him" (2:75). Unfortunately, however, "the least deserving in a commonwealth, are of all others most ambitious" (2:75), and the ambitions of these unworthy men, who usurp stations for which they are unfit, promote social chaos and ruin within the state. In "A Looking Glass for Christians," Smith elaborates:

> It is not meet that he should be a free-man which was never a prentice, nor that he should leap into Moses's chair that never sat at Gamaliel's feet. If thou doest never so well, and be not called to it, the Scripture saith straight, "Who hath required this of thee?" thou art an usurper of another's office. . . . We are compared to a body; some men are like the head, and they must rule; some are like the tongue, and they must teach; some are like the hand, and they must work. When this order is confounded, then that cometh to pass which we read of Eve; when the woman would lead her husband, both fell into the ditch. (1:478)

In the hierarchy of a kingdom, Smith regards the prince as the highest authority. He is not only head of the secular body of his kingdom but also the ecclesiastical. In *God's Arrow against Atheism and Irreligion*, Smith writes that "all the ancient churches have affirmed and acknowledged the supreme authority of princes above and over all, both priest and people" (2:428).

Observing in "The Affinity of the Faithful" that "Solomon calleth obedience the end of all, as though without obedience all were to no end," Smith preaches the doctrine of man's obedience to earthly rulers. In *God's Arrow*, he writes that "it is manifest, by the practice of the apostles, and all their precepts, commanding all Christians to obey their rulers, their kings, and princes, yea, though they were persecutors, that the apostles never had any such authority committed to them" [which would relieve them of their duty of obedience] (2:427).

Smith's thinking on the subject of obedience is in the tradition established by Augustine and Aquinas. Augustine, like Smith, regards the prince as a deputy elected by the Lord. He is God's annointed. To quote Herbert A. Deane's papaphrase of Augustine, "We must never forget that the wicked or unjust man who exercises rule is in every way as legitimate and as much entitled to absolute obedience as the most pious or just ruler. The goodness or badness, piety or impiety, justice or injustice of the ruler has nothing at all to do with his title to rule and to be obeyed."[27] Both Augustine and Aquinas insist that God must be obeyed first and earthly princes second. If an earthly prince commands his subject to act contrary to God's commandments, the subject must obey God and disobey the prince. Hence, perfect obedience, writes Aquinas, is obeying "all things lawful," as opposed to foolish obedience, "which obeys even in matters unlawful."[28] Reflecting this tradition, Smith writes in "The Affinity of the Faithful":

> When Paul said, "Children, obey your parents in the Lord," Eph. vi.1, he means not that we should obey them against the Lord. As when he saith, "Obey princes for conscience' sake", Rom. xiii.5, he meaneth not that we should obey them against conscience. Therefore, when it cometh to this, that the earthly father commandeth one thing, and the heavenly father commandeth another thing; then, as Peter answered the rulers, so mayest thou answer thy

---

[27]Herbert A. Deane, *The Political and Social Ideas of St. Augustine* (New York: Columbia University Press, 1963), p. 134.

[28]St. Thomas Aquinas, *Summa Theologica*, trans. Fathers of the English Dominican Province (New York: Benziger Brothers, Inc., 1947), 2-2, q. 104, a. 5.

> parents, "Whether is it meet to obey God or you?" Acts iv.19. (2:292)

Although Smith's remarks are chiefly directed to the relationship between parents and children, they have an obvious bearing on the relationship between subjects and rulers as well. One other passage which applies to the obedience of rulers as well as to parents might be cited:

> Three things children receive of their parents, life, maintenance, and instruction. For these three they owe other three; for life, they owe love; for maintenance, they owe obedience; for instruction, they owe reverence. For life, they must be loved as fathers; for maintenance, they must be obeyed as masters; for instruction, they must be reverenced as tutors. But as there is a King of kings, which must be obeyed above kings, so there is a Father of fathers, which must be obeyed above fathers. (2:293)

Obedience to God is man's duty which must never be neglected; it is the action with which God is well pleased. In his second sermon on "The Sinner's Confession," Smith writes:

> This was the fruit which it had in the heart of Zaccheus, namely, obedience to the voice of Christ, a fruit more precious and acceptable unto God than the most pleasant fruits which Eden yielded, and a sacrifice more sweet and acceptable unto him than all the sacrifices which the law required. This is "the sacrifice wherewith the Lord is pleased," Heb. xiii.16, even when his voice is obeyed, 1 Sam xv.22. (2:147)

Smith's view is that it is the duty of preachers to teach their congregations to render willing obedience to the princes of the world. According to Smith, the apostles of Christ set the example all men should follow, and preachers must not only practice obedience themselves but teach it to others. In *God's Arrow*, Smith writes:

> Their duty is rather to practice obedience themselves . . . and to teach the same obedience to others, as the apostles of Christ did. Yea, Christ himself said, "his kingdom was not of this world," John xviii.36; himself likewise refused to be made a king, John vi.15; himself paid tribute unto Caesar, and commanded others to give the same, and all other duties of subjection and obedience unto Caesar. (2:427)

Kings are not only the deputies elected by the lord, they are also, according to Smith, not subject to any earthly power. None is their superior; none has a lawful right to depose God's earthly rulers, for none can lay upon them the vesture of rule but God alone: "*Per me reges regnant, et principes dominantur*: 'By me kings reign, and princes bear dominion' " (2:426). In *God's Arrow against Atheism and Irreligion*, Smith attacks the Pope for exalting himself above princes:

> The church of Rome doth further hold, that their pope hath authority to depose kings and princes. But by what title? It is clear that in his either so doing, or attempting to do, he is both a notable traitor unto God, whose authority he doth claim and arrogate, and unto princes, to whom he should be subject. For the raising and pulling down of princes God hath reserved to himself alone in his power. For it is he, not the pope, that "deposeth the mighty from their seats, and exalteth them that are of low degree." (2:426)

According to Smith, kings are more obliged than anyone else to execute God's laws, for more than anybody else they bear the image of God. In "The Magistrates' Scripture," he cites Psalm 82:6, 7 for his text, in which kings are referred to as gods. Kings and other earthly rulers are called gods because God "hath given them power to speak to the people in his name, and to execute his judgment upon them. Out of this name rulers may learn how to govern, and subjects how to obey" (1:357). Viceroys bear a similar relationship to their king as their king bears to God. Smith writes, "As the inferior magistrates do nothing but as the superior magistrate prescribeth, so they which rule under God, for God, must rule by the prescript of God, and do nothing but as their conscience tells them that God would do himself" (1:357-58). In remarking on kings as gods, Smith says:

> Princes and rulers have many names of honour, but this is the honourablest name in their titles, that they are called gods; other names have been given them of men for reverence, or flattery, but no man could give them this name but God himself. Therefore their name is a glass wherein they may see their duty, how God doth honour them, and how they should honour him. (1:361-62)

As servants of God, kings not only should protect Christ's image on earth and promote the Christian religion at home and abroad but also represent in their own person Christ's example of humility. If the Son of God humbled himself to come down to earth from heaven, kings must set the example of true humility now that the Son has returned to heaven (1:294). Of all men they should be the most angelic; but, as Smith laments in "The Magistrates' Scripture," "for want of angels we are fain to make magistrates of men" (1:358). As men, kings often forget or willfully neglect their awesome responsibilities and appear to be the viceroys of Satan rather than of God. In "Paul and King Agrippa," Smith writes:

> Paul doth not wish Agrippa more honour, or more wealth, or more friends, but more religion, which is the greatest want of princes. Although they have received a kingdom, yet they are not so thankful as they which have received nothing but from hand to mouth. Though they have done a thousand times more evil, yet they are not so penitent as he which hath done least of all. They sit in God's seat, and are called gods, but are not like God, but like mammon, more than their names and their crowns. (1:450)

Instead of setting an example in humility, kings set examples in the worst of the seven deadly sins, pride. In his first sermon on "The Pride of Nebuchadnezzar," Smith writes:

> These are the meditations of princes and noblemen; when they behold their buildings, or open their coffers, or look upon their train swimming after them, they think as Nebuchadnezzar thought, "Is not this great Babel?" Is not this great glory? Is not this the train that maketh me reverenced in the streets? Are not these the things which shall make my children rich? Is not this the house that shall keep my name, and cause me to be remembered, and make them which are children now to speak of me hereafter? (1:175)

It is the preacher's duty to reprove kings who have fallen away from God. In a "A Caveat for Christians," Smith directly addresses those who preach and those who rule when he says, "so especially let him that ruleth, and him that teacheth, take heed lest he fall; for if the pillars shrink, the temple shakes" (2:37). Too many preachers, however, because of fear or for ambition's sake, direct their arrows of reproof so that they "glide by the faults of princes . . . ; [they] whisper behind their backs, as though they would reprove them if they durst, but for fear lest the prince, or councillor, or judge, or magistrate should take it as he means it, and think that he aims at them . . . , [they] speak in parables, as though they would cast a veil over their reproof, and eat their message before they have spoke it" (1:186). Smith, however, gives his "warning to all rulers, to put them in remembrance, that one Ruler is above, which must be served of them all, or else all their buildings, and treasures, and guards will not shield them from judgment when the stroke cometh, no more than they could save Nebuchadnezzar" (1:169).

Kings, according to Smith, should take special care to please God because they are more likely to be severely punished than common men. As they should be an example to all men of how to serve God, they will be made an example to all men of how God punishes those who fail to serve him. "Here is a glass for all the children of pride," writes Smith; "look upon Nebuchadnezzar, you that are great men like Nebuchadnezzar; for thus will God make his example of great men, because they should be examples to others" (1:198). God demands that the kings of the earth honor him as they demand that their subjects honor them, or "he will tread upon their crowns, and they shall hear . . . at last, 'Thy kingdom shall depart from thee' " (1:187). When the fatal hour comes to the king, "God takes him where he is pleasantest and lustiest, and safest, in his palace . . . as he took Herod when his guard stood by him, Acts xii.23, that he might see that nothing can guard him from God, but God must guard him from danger, or else princes be not safer than subjects" (1:183).

Although Smith never preaches against the Queen or her government, he is, nevertheless, not blind to the ills besetting the kingdom and its Church. The seven deadly sins seem to be contending one against another for first place in English hearts, and pride and avarice are always chief among the seven. Smith devotes two sermons to one kind of greed which he regards as a serious flaw in the garment of London life, as well as one of the principal evils of the age: usury. In addition to these two sermons, he alludes to this important subject in a number of others, always with the sharpest condemnation.

In his preface to "The Examination of Usury," he expresses the wish that he might "take but this one weed out of the Londoners' garden" (1:87). London seems to have been particularly infested with usurers; for, according to Smith, "it is said that there be more of this profession in this city, than there be in all the land beside" (1:89). After a brief introduction to his topic, Smith outlines his matter:

> First, I will define what usury is; secondly, I will shew you what usury doth signify; thirdly, I will shew the unlawfulness of it; fourthly, I will shew the kinds of it; fifthly, I will shew the arguments which are alleged for it; sixthly, I will shew the punishment of it; seventhly, I will shew you what opinion we should hold of them which do not lend upon usury, but borrow upon usury; lastly, I will shew you what they should do which have got their riches by usury. (1:89)

Smith's treatment of usury indicates the seriousness of the problem and Smith's reaction to it. His definition of usury is "that gain which is gotten by lending . . . ; [the usurer] receive[s] more than was borrowed; and therefore one calls the usurer a legal thief, because before he steals, he tells the party how much he will steal, as though he stole by the law" (1:89). Smith points out how the rich usurers live off the poor of the land; how, like large fish devouring small, they devour the helpless; how they are the most uncharitable of men (1:91); how they are like ivy on a tree: "The ivy claspeth the oak like a lover, but it claspeth out all the juice and sap, that the oak cannot thrive after it; so the usurer lendeth like a friend, but he covenanteth like an enemy; for he claspeth the borrower with such bonds, that ever after he diminisheth as fast as the usurer increaseth" (1:92-93).

Smith contemns usurers of all kinds, sparing none, but borrowing from usurers he hesitatingly approves, for "the Scripture seemeth to forbid taking, but not giving [usury]" (1:105). He refuses, however, to attempt to resolve the right or the wrong of the question, leaving the onus upon the conscience of those thus engaged. But Smith writes:

> [I]f some should come unto me in that necessity and extremity which I can imagine, and ask, May I borrow money of these usurers to save my life, or my credit, or my living, seeing no man will lend me freely? I would answer him as the prophet answered Naaman, neither Do, nor Do not, but "Go in peace." I will not forbid thee, nor will I condemn thee; but if thy conscience condemn thee not, I think thy sin one of the least sins; and as Naaman prayed, "Lord, be merciful unto me in this," 2 Kings v.18, so I think the Lord will be merciful unto thee in this. But if thy conscience go against it, then do it not, for it is sin to thee, though it be free for another. (1:105)

Thus, Smith writes, "I would have no man pay interest unto usurers but for necessity, even as a traveller giveth his purse unto a thief because he cannot choose" (1:106). He concludes that those who have acquired riches by usury are obliged to return that profit to the rightful owners or their heirs, if salvation is to be hoped for. If such an act be impossible, that is, if the rightful owners be dead and with them their heirs, then Smith requires the usurer to give his profits to the poor, "for they are the next heirs" (1:108). The Church, however, cannot accept the profits of this ill-gotten usury, for "it is not lawful for us to apply the gain of our ill-gotten goods to the service of God" (2:156). Yet total restoration of profits is not enough to win the approbation of God and to bring the usurer to salvation. The restoration must be accompanied by a willing heart, for his gift is worth nothing if it comes not from a willing mind (2:119). In "The Benefit of Contentation," Smith states that few sins are as destructive as covetousness and the love of money:

> For what hath brought usury, and simony, and bribery, and cruelty, and subtilty, and envy, and strife, and deceit into this city, and made every house an inn, and every shop a market of oaths, and lies, and fraud, but the superflous love of money? Name covetousness, and thou hast named the mother of all these mischiefs. (2:272-73)

In addition to covetousness, Smith preaches specifically against the mother of the deadly sins, namely, pride, which is always in the forefront of the world's evils. He has a number of sermons on pride in its most damning form, such as the deep-rooted pride of kings like Nebuchadnezzar. But he also detects pride in its less serious forms, too, even in such venial eccentricities as one's wardrobe. Although Smith reproves the vanity of dress and fine clothing, he knows that one need not be rich or beautiful or learned to be vain. Admittedly, "pride hath worse children than vanity of apparel," Smith concedes in "A Dissuasion from Pride, and an Exhortation to Humility": "Tyranny in princes, ambition in nobles, rebellion in subjects, disobedience in children, stubbornness in servants; name pride," says Smith, "and thou hast named their mother" (1:209). Nevertheless, vanity in clothing is sinful and should be accordingly admonished. Women especially fall into this vanity. Smith, a lifelong bachelor, remarks thus on the subject:

> This is their work as soon as they rise, to put a pedlar's shop upon their backs, and colour their faces, and prick their ruffs, and frizzle their hair, and then their day's work is done, as though their office were to paint a fair image every morning, and at night to blot it out again. (1:207)[29]

Fashionable women are not alone, however, in being sinfully vain of their apparel. Once such vanity was confined largely to the courts of kings, but now, laments Smith, "it is crept into every house" (1:207). London is in love with fashion, and so contagious is that vanity that, if Pride herself should walk the streets attired in her vainest apparel, "she would even go like many in the streets, for she could not go braver, nor look stouter, nor mince finer, nor set on more laces, nor make larger cuts, nor carry more trappings about her, than our ruffians and wantons do at this day" (1:207).[30] And

---

[29]Cf. "The Pride of Nebuchadnezzar" (1:175). Cf. "A Dissuasion from Pride, and an Exhortation to Humility" (1:205).

[30]Cf. Smith's reiteration of this point in "The Trial of Vanity," 1:382: "And yet there are more vanities in our apparel, ruff upon ruff, lace upon lace, cut

everyone—male and female alike— is attempting to outshine the other. Smith observes:

> [T]hey disguise their bodies so, till they know not themselves; for the servant goeth like the master, the hand-maid like her mistress, the subject like the prince, as though he had forgotten his calling, and mistook himself, like a man in the dark, which puts on another man's coat for his own, that is too wide . . . for his body; so unmeet for their calling, so contrary to nature, that I cannot call them fitter than the monsters of apparel. (1:207)

Pride, of course, is the "deviser of all these vanities, which now neither shame, nor laws, nor preaching can take away" (1:208). It is hard to determine whether the apparel makes the mind puff up with pride or whether the mind is vain already. At any rate, says Smith, "It is a wonder to see how a gay coat, or a gold ring, or a wrought handkerchief can brave a man's mind, that he thinks better of himself that day when he weareth them than any day else, and speaks, and walks, and look after another fashion than he did before" (1:208). These are not by any means the limits of man's vanity; they merely hint at a vast reservoir, for the vanities of ancient times live on. In "The Trial of Vanity," Smith notes:

> For are not many vain in their knowledge, vain in their policies, vain in their learning, as others are vain in their ignorance: Was not the wisdom of Ahithophel a vain thing? the swiftness of Asahel a vain thing? the strength of Goliath a vain thing? the treasures of Nebuchadnezzar a vain thing? the honour of Haman a vain thing? the beauty of Absalom a vain thing? the knowledge of the scribes a vain thing? the devotion of the pharisees a vain thing? And so is the learning of all those a vain thing that do no good with it. (1:377)

---

upon cut, four and twenty orders, to the third and fourth degree, as though our apparel were apparelled, until the woman be not worth so much as her attire; that if we would see vanity herself, how she would go if she did wear apparel, she would even go like our women; for she could not go, not speak, nor look vainer. Who doth not know that . . . there is a heart within, vainer than the apparel is without?"

Where better than in the Church might the vanities of dress be more readily observed? Not completely damning in themselves, vanities in their less serious forms—vanities of wardrobe, of strength, of learning, etc.—are symptomatic of the more deadly kinds of pride. Smith is perfectly aware that the mind which is distracted by frivolous vanities from the important concerns of the soul is in great danger of losing the soul in the end to the world and the devil. One need not be a villain to forfeit the reward of eternal peace with God.

One of Smith's chief concerns as a preacher is to teach men that it is usually the small, seemingly harmless acts and negligences, not the great cardinal sins, that snare the soul and damn it at last. He urges his congregation again and again to heed God's word and to live upright and honest lives. Unfortunately, however, few profit from such advice. One reason, according to Smith, that such inordinate numbers fail in their Christian commitment is that they simply do not hear God's word as it is preached to them. So seriously does Smith regard mental and spiritual deafness that he ranks them as two of the principal adversaries of Christ's Church.

He devotes two complete sermons to the problem of inattentiveness in church and frequently refers to it in others. He is fully aware that many attend church services for reasons other than for their soul's sake. In his first sermon on "The Art of Hearing," he enumerates some of the more common reasons why Elizabethans attended church:

> [S]ome come unto the service to save forfeiture, and then they stay the sermon for shame; some come because they would not be accounted atheists; some come because they would avoid the name of papists; some come to please their friends . . . ; some come with their masters and mistresses for attendance; some come with a flame; they have heard great speech of the man, and therefore they will spend one hour to hear him once, but to see whether it be so as they say; some come because they be idle . . . ; another hath some occasion of business, and he appoints his friends to meet him at such a sermon, as they do at Paul's. (1:326-27)

Once at the service, their various motives make it difficult for some in the congregation to be attentive of the preacher's sermon; many listen only in part and lose the kernel while they gather the chaff. Smith categorizes them thus:

> [O]ne is like an Athenian, and he harkeneth after news; if the preacher say anything of our armies beyond the sea, or council at home, or matters at court, that is his lure. Another is like the pharisee, and he watcheth if anything be said that may be wrested to be spoken against persons in high place, that he may play the devil in accusing of his brethren; let him write that in his tables too. Another smacks of eloquence, and he gapes for a phrase, that when he cometh to his ordinary he may have one figure more to grace and worship his table. Another is malcontent, and he never pricketh up his ears till the preacher come to gird against some whom he spiteth, and when the sermon is done, he remembereth nothing which was said to him, but that which was spoken against others. Another cometh to gaze about the church; he hath an evil eye, which is still looking upon that from which Job did avert his eye. Another cometh to muse; so soon as he is set, he falleth into a brown study; sometimes his mind runs on his market, sometimes on his journey, sometimes of his suit, sometimes of his dinner, sometimes of his sport after dinner, and the sermon is done before the man thinks where he is. Another cometh to hear, but so soon as the preacher hath said his prayer, he falls fast asleep, as though he had been brought in for a corpse, and the preacher should preach at his funeral. (1:327)

Like Mary, who sat at the feet of Jesus and listened to his teaching, many sit at the feet of preachers; but they, unlike Mary, are asleep. Smith finds it necessary to reprove some in the congregation for physically falling asleep in church, warning that "he which leaneth his ears on his pillow, goeth home again like the child which he leadeth in his hand, and scarce remembereth the preacher's text" (1:321). Too many are like Jonah, for they sleep when they need most to be aware and eager to learn God's will for their lives (1:241).

In Smith's third sermon on Jonah, part of the text includes the shipmaster's words to the sleeping Jonah, "What meanest thou, O sleeper? arise and call upon thy God." When Smith reaches that part of the text in his sermon, he sounds almost as if he might be talking to someone who is literally asleep at that moment in the church, and he appears to use the text as a means of waking him. He urges:

> Many of you come to hear the word, and here you fall asleep when you have most need to be waking; but I am glad I have now gotten a text to waken you, for now I cannot read my text but I must say, "What meanest thou, O sleeper? arise?" But I pray you, have I not wakened you, and yet you sleep again? If you mark not what is said unto you, you are asleep, though your eyes be open. But if you were as wise as Jonah, you would not sleep here in the sight of all the people, but would rather get you to sleep in some corner; for Jonah went under the hatches to sleep, and would not sleep in the sight of the mariners. If you were as wise a Jonah, you would thank him that wakened you, as no doubt Jonah did. . . . You would all be found in the church when the Lord cometh, but you would not be found sleeping in the church. (2:245)

Smith's meaning of *sleep* always broadens, however, to include those who are asleep spiritually: usurers, extortioners, drunkards, blasphemers—all who are deaf to the teachings of Jesus Christ. He reminds them that, whether their sleep be physical or spiritual, it cannot go unseen by God, even though they may fool men. He warns, "You are watched, though I see you not below; and none of you can steal a nap, and not be espied . . . ; I can as well stand in the pulpit unseen, as you can sit and sleep there and not be espied" (2:245-46). Sadly, when men wake, they often wake to wrong concerns. Instead of heeding their soul's need, instead of fearing eternal damnation, instead of yearning for the upright heart and pure, they argue endlessly about set prayers, about saints' days, about fasting, about clerical vestments. Nothing has importance, nor should be of concern, until the soul be safe. Only then, warns Smith, is man at liberty to inquire into less significant matters.

Smith preaches for the reformation of the Church, but his perspective is wide; he refuses to settle for a surface reformation only. He wants the Church to reform at the core, to purify itself in the deepest sense by placing into proper perspective that which is essential to salvation. In his comprehensive understanding of the problems of the English church, he resembles Richard Hooker, who writes in *Of Laws of Ecclesiastical Polity*: "I wish that men would give themselves to meditate what we have by the sacrament and less to dispute of the manner how." Henry Smith is of like mind. Although he objects to certain rituals in his Church, he recognizes that the symbol is never so important as the thing symbolized; he, consequently, preaches for reforms which will not rend the fabric of the Church. Arguments about vestments, set prayers, saints' days, and other such matters of Church discipline, he urges, must never assume an importance above doctrine, nor may the one ever be mistaken for the other, except at one's own peril. In *God's Arrow against Atheism and Irreligion*, he writes:

> [T]his desired discipline is not an essential part of the church; for it doth resemble the wall of a city, or an hedge or ditch about a vineyard; and it is a city, though the walls be wanting, and it is a vineyard, though the hedge or ditch be wanting; though so much the less fortified, I grant. Inasmuch therefore as we have the preaching of God's holy word, and the right administration of the sacraments, which be the essential marks of the true church, none ought to forsake our church for any other defect, corruption, or imperfection. (2:447)

Smith censures those who would destroy Christ's true Church because of a few set prayers, saints' days, and the like. He minces no words when he writes in *God's Arrow*:

> Let them [i.e., the Brownists and Barrowists] no longer for shame charge our church with idolatry, except they were better able to prove it, which neither they nor all the world shall do. To say, as they say, that a set form of prayer is used in the church and exhibited unto God, the prayer being framed according to the rule of God's word, is idolatry, is detestable; for by as good reason they may condemn all prayer made to God by the preacher or pastor of the congregation, which they will not do; and besides, all the

> reformed churches in Christendom have a set form of public prayers for public meetings and congregations. (2:448)[31]

Equally shallow and deluded is the reasoning of those who accuse the English church of idolatry because it keeps saints' days and names its churches after saints. Smith argues:

> They say that we observe saints' days, and dedicate churches unto them; but they should shew that we do these things in honour of the saints, else have they no reason to charge our church with idolatry, as wickedly they do; for the statute itself doth express, that our church doth call them holidays, not for the saints' sake, but for the holy exercises used upon them in the public assemblies. Again, true it is, that divers amongst us are called by the names of those saints they are dedicated unto; but to say, therefore we do dedicate churches unto them, it is very ridiculous. For when we call St. Peter's church or St. Paul's church, it is but to distinguish them from other churches by their names. (2:448-49)

Smith conceives the real reason for the English church's observance of days of fast to be economic; at the same time, he puts in a barb against the Catholics:

> Moreover, it is true, that we observe fasting days; but therein we observe no Romish fasts, nor place therein the worship of God, nor the remission of our sins, nor the merit of eternal life, as the papists do. But the politic laws of this land, which appoint that men shall not eat flesh upon certain days, do it in respect of the commonwealth, as to maintain navigation so much the better, and for spare of the breed of young cattle, appointing moreover a penalty for such as shall take the days to be observed as meritorious Romish fasts. (2:449)

Of vestments, Smith is less tolerant. He considers them a symbol of Rome, and he has an intense distrust of anything Catholic. In "The True Trial of the Spirits," he writes:

> But if we be not idolaters, yet we have the show of idolatry. If we be not of antichrist's religion, yet we are of antichrist's fashion, so long

---

[31]Cf. "The True Trial of the Spirits," 1:143: "Hath it not the shew of error to say that no man may use any set prayer seeing there be many set prayers, and psalms, and blessings in the holy Scripture, which were used in the same form?"

> as we have the same vestures, and the same orders, and the same titles that antichrist knoweth his ministers by. It is said that the serpent's sting is in her tail, and so it seems; for this tail of antichrist (which the pope hath left behind him like an evil savour) is unto us as the remnant of the Canaanites were unto the Jews, Num. xxxiii.55. They should have destroyed all the Canaanites, but because they spared some, therefore they whom they left were goads in their sides and pricks in their eyes, that they could never be in quiet for them. So we should have expelled the head and the tail too of antichrist; but because we did not, therefore the remnants of popery are goads in our sides and pricks in our eyes, that we cannot yet be in quiet for them. Therefore let us pray that he which hath taken away the evil, will take away the show of evil too. (1:143-44)

Although Smith is acutely aware of the shortcomings of the Church of England and preaches sharply against them, urging always for reform, he cannot abide a break in the Church. All changes, he thinks, can be effected in time, but they must be effected within the Established Church. Such are the limits of Smith's Puritanism: he ceases to be sympathetic with the aims of any reforming party as soon as it advocates breaking away from the Church of England, thinking itself capable of working for changes, however noble, outside the established framework. Of the Separatists, Smith writes at the end of *God's Arrow against Atheism and Irreligion*:

> I therefore wish them to cease their slander against this church and to cease their damnable schism, and to be reconciled to that church of ours, from whence they have foolishly departed; for how imperfect a church soever it be,—whose imperfections God cure in his good time,—yet shall they never be able to shew otherwise, but that the Church of England is the true church of God, from which it is utterly unlawful to make a separation. (2:449)

Thus Smith inveighed against Brownists, Barrowists, and Separatists of all kinds, regarding them all as thoughtless dissenters whose actions were not only a damnation to themselves but also a blow against Christ and his church. Condemning them one and all, even though they were often attempting to bring about the very changes that he recognized as desirable, Smith insisted on the soundness of the English church and regarded it as the only means whereby Englishmen might learn about God's plan of salvation.

In Chapter 6 of *God's Arrow against Atheism and Irreligion*, Smith writes about the reformation of the Church, especially when it is attempted by schism, stating his own position in clear terms:

> Many there be who, out of a godly and zealous mind, do in good sort seek reformation, and for that church government, which Christ himself hath instituted in his church, whom I neither dare nor do reprove. Others there be, that seek reformation amiss, with venomous and slanderous tongues, railing and reviling against those which understand it. Which things do neither grace themselves, nor yet the cause which they would prefer. Other some there be, who, to make the cause of reformation odious, do say, that it abolished her majesty's supreme government, and authority in causes ecclesiastical. (2:446-47)

Smith is here again of the mind of the greater ecclesiastic, Richard Hooker, who wrote in *Of Laws of Ecclesiastical Polity* that "There will come a time when three words uttered with charity and meekness shall receive a far more blessed reward than three thousand volumes written with disdainful sharpness of wit." Similarly, in *God's Arrow*, Smith writes:

> I would wish all men to speak the truth, and to seek the preferment of God's truth, in a dutiful, peaceable, and charitable sort. Let the cause be made no worse than it is. For my part, I desire no more than every Christian ought, namely, that the truth of God should carry the pre-eminence, whatever it be. And I would to God that, all malice and contention set apart, all of all parts would grow more charitably affected, both in their words and in their writings, one towards another; for so would this controversy sooner come to an end, and the more speedily be decided. Others there be, who for that in so long time they cannot see their desired discipline and church government to be established, run from our church, and make a schism and separation from us, erecting discipline by their own authority, condemning our church to be no church, that that may make their detestable schism the more allowable. These are the Brownists and Barrowists. (2:447)

In the same treatise, Smith draws an analogy between the Church of England and a man with one leg:

> [I]f a man lose a leg or arm, yet none will deny him to be a man for all this blemish or defect; yea, though he put a wooden leg instead of his leg which he wanteth, yet he remaineth a man still, because his principal parts remain; so though we want that discipline, yet we have the principal parts of the church, namely, the right preaching of the word of God and administration of the sacraments, and therefore a true church of God undoubtedly. And if we have a true church, though not a perfect church, let the Brownists and Barrowists consider from whence they are fallen; for if the church of Christ be the body of Christ, as St. Paul affirmeth, what do they else but by their schism and separation rent themselves from the body of Christ? (2:448)

Whatever Smith's subject—whether an indictment against Brownists and Barrowists, an exhortation for obedience, or advice on the nursing of babies—he employs established formats. Elizabethan preachers had three prevalent sermon forms from which to choose: "the 'ancient' form, the new Reformed arrangement of Doctrines and Uses, and the 'modern' style so modified as to approximate to the true classical form with its variations."[32] Smith is particularly attracted to two of these forms, the "ancient" and the "modern." The "ancient" form, which is extensively used in the homilies of the Church of England, is employed in almost half of his sermons.[33] It has no elaborate scheme, or arrangement, but consists primarily of an "explication and application of a passage of Scripture (often the

---

[32]J. W. Blench, *Preaching in England in the Late Fifteenth and Sixteenth Centuries* (Oxford: Basil Blackwell, 1964), p. 100.

[33]According to Blench, the following of Smith's sermons are in the "ancient" form: "The Christian's Sacrifice," "The True Trial of the Spirits," "The Wedding Garment," "The Way to Walk In," "The Honour of Humility," "The Young Man's Task," "The Christian's Practice," "The Art of Hearing" (2), "The Trial of Vanity," "The Banquet of Job's Children," "A Caveat for Christians," "A Memento for Magistrates," "The Lawyer's Question," "The Lawgiver's Answer," "The Censure of Christ upon the Answer," "Two Sermons of the Song of Simeon," "The Calling of Jonah," "Jonah's Punishment," "The Trumpet of the Soul," "Mary's Choice," "The Benefit of Contentation," "The Affinity of the Faithful," and "The Lost Sheep Is Found" (n. 256, p. 101).

Gospel or Epistle of the Day), *secundum ordinem textus;* or of the topical treatment of any subject, according to reason and Scripture."[34] Smith's "The Wedding Garment" is in the "ancient" form. The text of the sermon is Romans 13:14, "Put ye on the Lord Jesus Christ." The sermon is essentially no more than an explication of the biblical text and an application of it to daily life. He begins his sermon thus:

> I have chosen a text which is the sum of the Bible. For all Scripture runneth upon Christ, like the title of a book, because he is Alpha and Omega, Rev. i.8, the beginning and the end of man's salvation; therefore he is figured in the law, foretold in the prophets, and fulfilled in the gospel. Some places point to his divinity, some to his humanity, some to his kingdom, some to his priesthood, some to his prophecy, some to his conception, some to his birth, some to his life, some to his miracles, some to his passion, some to his resurrection, some to his ascension, some to his glorification; all point to the Saviour, like John Baptist, when he said, 'This is the Lamb of God, which taketh away the sins of the world,' John i.20. Therefore learn Christ and learn all. (1:147)

After thoroughly explicating the Scripture and applying it to his congregation, he ends as follows:

> Thus have you heard what is meant by putting on Christ: first, to clothe ourselves with righteousness and holiness like Christ; and then, because our own righteousness is too short to cover our arms, and legs, and thighs of sin, but still some bare place will peer out, and shame us in the sight of God, therefore we must borrow Christ's garments, as Jacob did his brother's, Gen. xxvii.15, and cover ourselves with his righteousness; that is, believe that his righteousness shall supply our unrighteousness, and his sufferings shall stand for our sufferings, because he came to fulfill the law, and bear the curse, and satisfy his Father for us, that all which believe in him might not die, but have life everlasting, John iii.16. Now I have shewed you this goodly garment, you must go to another to help you to put it on; and none can put this garment upon you, but he which is the garment, the Lord Jesus Christ. (1:157)

[34]Ibid., pp. 71-72.

Smith also makes extensive use of what J. W. Blench calls the "modern" form. Blench describes the form thus:

> The 'modern' style consists of the following parts: the Theme; the Exordium or Protheme or Antetheme; the Prayer; the Introduction of the Theme; the Division (with or without Subdivision); and lastly the Discussion. Of these, the Exordium, Protheme or Antetheme may be omitted, while the Introduction of the Theme is not found in later practice. The Theme is a text from Scripture, from which three main ideas may be extracted, and it forms the basis of the sermon. The Exordium which leads to a bidding Prayer . . . is based either on part of the main Theme not to be treated in the body of the sermon, or on another text, the Protheme or Antetheme, allied to the main Theme by one of its words. After the Prayer, the Theme is again given out for the benefit of latecomers, and the preacher . . . proceeds to the proper Introduction of the Theme, by Narration or Argumentation. . . . Then follows the Division of the Theme into three parts. . . . Each part of the Division must be supported by other scriptural authorities. . . . These parts are either simply amplified, or from them comes the Subdivision.[35]

Professor Blench has extensively analyzed Smith's "A Preparative to Marriage" as an example of a sermon cast in the "modern" form. For the analysis, I refer you to his valuable study, *Preaching in England in the Late Fifteenth and Sixteenth Centuries*.[36]

Smith's personal touch is not to be found in his sermon forms, for in every instance he is conventional; however, in style and

---

[35]Ibid., pp. 72-73.

[36]Ibid., pp. 103-105. Cf. Blench, n. 279, p. 105, where he cites a number of Smith's sermons as representative of the "modern" form or adaptations of it. Among them are the following: "A Treatise on the Lord's Supper in Two Sermons," "The Examination of Usury in Two Sermons," "The Pride of Nebuchadnezzar," "The Fall of Nebuchadnezzar," "The Restitution of Nebuchadnezzar," "The Trial of the Righteous," "The Pilgrim's Wish," "The Godly Man's Request," "A Glass for Drunkards," "The Art of Hearing" (1), "The Heavenly Thrift," "The Magistrates' Scripture," "The Ladder of Peace," "The Betraying of Christ," "The Petition of Moses," "The Dialogue Between Paul and Agrippa," "The Humility of Paul," "A Looking-Glass for Christians," "Food for New-Born Babes," "Satan's Compassing the Earth," "The Poor Man's Tears,"

manner, his individuality and personality reveal themselves. In "The True Trial of the Spirits," Smith says that "to preach simply is not to preach rudely, nor unlearnedly, nor confusedly, but to preach plainly and perspicuously, that the simplest man may understand what is taught, as if he did hear his name" (1:139). Here Smith might be describing his own method of preaching; for simplicity and clarity, characteristics which undoubtedly contributed to his great popularity in the sixteenth century and later, are his trademarks. Thomas Smith, the general editor of the 1866 edition of Smith's sermons, observes: "So free are they from the affectations that disfigure most of the pulpit productions of the time, that there is scarcely an expression that would require alteration in order to adapt them to the tastes of the present day" (1:xx). The editor evaluates his style accurately; for Smith's work, lucid in every respect, can be read with with pleasure and ease even today. Smith's editor also remarks that the sermons "probably do not contain a dozen words that would not be understood by an ordinary modern audience; there is scarcely a pun or a play upon words from the beginning to the end of them" (1:xx). His dislike of affected, pompous language probably contributed to his sermons being used as a family book in many Elizabethan homes; for, as Bishop Fuller writes, "That these sermons have been used as a handmaid to prayer bedward in some families, is not unknown" (1:xx).

Although learned, Smith never makes an ostentatious display of knowledge in his sermons. His work is almost completely free of classical and mythological allusions, largely free, in fact, of references to profane literature of any kind. Even his use of the Church Fathers is not extensive; however, the few sermons in which he mentions them show that Smith knew them well. He supports almost all of his arguments with Scriptural references alone. For example, in his

---

"An Alarum from Heaven," "Jacob's Ladder," "The Sinner's Conversion," "The Sinner's Confession," "The Rebellion of Jonah," "The Sinful Man's Search," "Noah's Drunkenness."

first sermon on "A Treatise on the Lord's Supper," he writes: "To end this controversy [on transubstantiation] . . . , we need not go to any other expositor than Christ himself" (1:50). Such is Smith's general approach. Occasionally, however, when the additional support of the Church Fathers appears helpful to his case, he is capable of rising to the demand. For instance, in supplying additional support for his arguments regarding the body and blood of Christ, he writes: "I did not allege the Fathers in my sermon; but if any suspend his assent till they bring in their verdict, let him hear them make confession of their belief" (1:51). Smith then quotes from Augustine, Tertullian, Ambrose, Theodoret, Origen, Irenaeus, Cyril, Cyprian, Athanasius, and Chrysostom.

The work in which Smith incorporates the most extensive range of his learning is *God's Arrow against Atheism and Irreligion*, where he discloses not only his acquaintance with the Church Fathers but also with pagan philosophers. There, also, in an effort to set Christianity off as the true religion of the one true God, he reveals his knowledge of history and historians, as well as religious works outside the Christian domain. Among the ancient authorities, both pagan and Christian, whom Smith cites are Protagoras, Diagoras, Cicero, Seneca, Zeno, Aristotle, Plato, Theophrastus, Aphrodiseus, Plutarch, Epictetus, Socrates, Pythagoras, Architas, Tarentinus, Mercurius, Trismegistus, Persius, Herodotus, Polydor Virgil, Juvenal, Pliny, Tertullian, Tacitus, Homer, Hesiodus, Josephus, Eusebius, and a host of others.

Smith's knowledge of ancient languages is also disclosed in his sermons, but foreign phrases appear only rarely, never for ornament, but always to clarify and support. His most extensive use of the learned languages is in *God's Arrow*. Seldom, however, does he use a foreign expression without also giving its translation, as if he would have no one miss the point of his argument because of ignorance of foreign tongues. In many of his sermons, he also gives the original meaning of proper biblical names. For example, in his first sermon on "The Sinner's Conversion," he notes that *Zaccheus* means *simple, pure, honest* (2:136); in "An Alarum from Heaven," that the Greek word *baptisma* "doth not signify only a dipping, but such a dipping in the water as doth cleanse the party dipped" (2:61); in "The Sweet Song of Old Father Simeon," that *Isaac* signifies *laughter*, "whereby was shewed what joy and laughter there should be about Christ Jesus" (2:167); in "The Punishment of Jonah," that *Jonah* signifies a *dove* (2:207), (2:242); in "The Calling of Jonah," that the name of Jonah's father, *Amittai*, means *truth* (2:207) and that *Nineveh* means *beautiful* (2:210); in "Paul and King Agrippa," that "they which descant upon his name do note that *Agrippa* is as much as *Aegre paris*, which signifies him which hardly laboureth, and brings forth with pain, as Agrippa did" (1:441).

When Smith incorporates Latin and other languages into his sermons, he translates them immediately, with few exceptions, even when the foreign expressions are elementary. In his first sermon on "The Art of Hearing," Smith writes, "Christ calleth the word which we should hear, *verbum regni*, 'the word of the kingdom . . . ;' the disciples call the word which we should hear, *verbum vitae*, 'the word of life' "; in "Jacob's Ladder; or, The Way to Heaven," Smith calls the steps of the ladder "*Mature, propere, recte, constanter;* that is, *Begin betime, Make haste, Keep the way, and Hold to the end*" (2:83); in his first sermon on "The Lawyer's Question," he quotes the epicure who says, "*Ede, bibe, lude*, etc., or, as it is said, 'Let us eat and drink, for to-morrow we shall die' " (2:106).[37] Smith is unwilling to risk being misunderstood, unwilling to display his knowledge for fear that one simple soul might thereby stumble and miss the way to eternal life.

---

[37]Other examples of Smith's use of foreign languages are the following: In "The Lawgiver's Answer," he renders *In amore nihil amari* as "in love there is not mistake" (2:117); in his second sermon on "The Sweet Song of Old Father Simeon," he writes that "all things that are written are come to *Scriptum est, et factum est;* that is, as sure as it is written, so surely doth it come to pass" (2:193); in *God's Arrow*, Smith quotes freely and often from the ancients, but he is careful to translate even here in his most scholarly treatise. For example, he quotes from Plato's epistle to Dionysius: "*Hinc disces tu scribam ego serio necne; cum serio, ordior*

However commodious the scope of Smith's learning, however able he was to adorn his sermons with pagan philosophy, historical allusions, and the authoritative dicta of the Church Fathers, his abilities are never sanctioned by desire. His aim is never merely to inform his hearers, but always to reform them, nor does he ever forget his goal. All of the tools of rhetoric have but one end for him: clarification of thought. Toward that end, he uses a number of devices with especial frequency. The most frequently employed is the "as . . . so" construction which abounds in every sermon. For example, in his second sermon on "The Examination of Usury," Smith compares the usurer to a camel: "*As* a camel, when he comes home, casteth off his burden at the door, that he may enter into his stable; *so* they which are laden with other men's goods, when they go to heaven, must leave their burden where they had it, lest they be too gross to get in at the narrow gate" (1:107). In "The Pilgrim's Wish," he compares the true Christian to Noah's dove: "As the dove found no rest until she came to the ark, Gen. viii.9, *so* the faithful find no rest till they come to Christ" (1:265). In "The Way to Walk In," Smith compares the glutton's stomach to a watery ground: "*As* the moist and waterish grounds bring forth nothing but frogs and toads, *so* the belly and waterish stomach that is stuffed like a tun,

---

epistolam ab uno deo; cum secus a pluribus. Hereby, saith he, you shall know whether I write in earnest or not; for when I write in earnest, I begin my letter with one god, and when I write not in earnest, I do begin my letter in the name of many gods" (2:385); he quotes Tertullian: "*Verum quod primum, quod posterius adulterium est;* that is true whatsoever is first, and that is adulterate which is not the first" (2:396); he quotes Chrysostom's comment on the sinful woman of Canaan, who came to Christ: "*En prudentiam hujus mulieris; non precatur Jacobum, non supplicat Johanni, non adit ad Petrum, nec apostolorum coetum respicit, aut ullum eorum, requirit; sed pro his omnibus poenitentiam sibi comitem adjungit et ad ipsum fontem progreditur:* Behold the wisdom of this woman; she doth not pray James, she doth not beseech John, she goeth not to Peter, she looketh not to the company of the apostles, neither doth request of any of them, but for all this she taketh repentance for her companion, and goeth to the very fountain itself" (2:436).

bringeth forth nothing but a drowsy mind, foggy thoughts, filthy speeches, and corrupt affections" (1:163). Writing of the apostle Paul in "The Pilgrim's Wish," Smith compares God to water: "*As* no water could quench his thirst until he drank of the water of life, and then he thirsted no more; *so* nothing can fill the soul which was made for God, but God alone" (1:264). Finally, in "The Christian's Practice," Smith uses a kind of double simile to talk about knowledge and righteousness: "*As* the water engendereth ice, and the ice again engendereth water, *so* knowledge begets righteousness, and righteousness again begetteth knowledge" (1:252).[38]

Another rhetorical device—or "annoying trick," according to Alan Herr—which Smith employs, at times with greater frequency than skill, is his use of "that is" to clarify a point that is already obvious. In "A Preparative to Marriage," he writes:

> So, if Christ be at your marriage, *that is*, if you marry in Christ, your water shall be turned into wine; *that is*, your peace, and your rest . . . shall begin with your marriage; but if you marry not in Christ, then your wine shall be turned into water: *That is*, you shall live worse hereafter than you did before [Italics mine]. (1:6)

It is likely that, when Smith preached from the pulpit, his manner and intonation rendered such stylistic eccentricities palatable; but in their printed form such expression as " 'Woe to him that is alone,' that is, he which is alone shall have woe" (1:12) soon tire the reader.

Smith is also fond of subordinate clauses. As Thomas K. Ehret points out, "If a reader examines the opening 100 lines of 'The Godly Man's Request,' for example, he will find approximately two subordinate clauses for every independent clause."[39] What is true of "The Godly Man's Request" is true of most of Smith's sermons. Ehret evaluates Smith's weakness in the use of subordinate clauses

---

[38]For other examples of Smith's use of the "as . . . so" construction, see 1:350; 1:351; 1:353; 1:394; 1:400; 1:401; 1:404; 1:441; 2:87; 2:119; 2:207; 2:231; 2:293; 2:361.

[39]Thomas King Ehret, *Four Sermons of Henry Smith*, p. lix.

as representative of a greater weakness in the logical development of the sermons themselves. He writes:

> I question whether so much subordination enhances a prose style: one sometimes loses track of which *which* is modifying what *what*! Indeed, the weaknesses in Smith's syntax are indicative of the weakness of the sermons as a whole. One is carried along by clusters of dependent clauses and suddenly perturbed by what these modifiers are relating to. In the same way, one is swept away by passages on death in *The Magistrate's Scripture* only to realize that these passages do not relate particularly to magistrates but to all men. There is, in short, a frequent lack of tight unity, an artistic clarity of purpose.[40]

Ehret's assessment is essentially valid; Smith's prose does carry one along with a rapidity that hinders close examination of subject matter; frequently he even achieves a hypnotic effect by repetition. Note, for example, the following passage from "The Trial of Vanity":

> For are not many *vain* in their knowledge, *vain* in their policies, *vain* in their learning, as others are *vain* in their ignorance? Was not the wisdom of Ahithophel a *vain* thing? the swiftness of Asahel a *vain* thing? the strength of Goliath a *vain* thing? the treasures of Nebuchadnezzar a *vain* thing? the honour of Haman a *vain* thing? the beauty of Absalom a *vain* thing? the knowledge of the scribes a *vain* thing? the devotion of the pharisees a *vain* thing? (1:377)

Smith also uses bold and unusual images, many of them taken directly from the Bible, to drive home a point. For instance, he admonishes the Christian to hold to the straight and narrow way and to "let the dog turn to the vomit, and the swine to the wallow" (2:92). He compares truth in wicked man to a jewel "on a stinking dunghill" (2:129). In "The Wedding Garment," he compares man's righteousness to a menstrual cloth, "which had more need to be washed itself, than to wipe that which is foul" (1:153); and in his second sermon on "The Art of Hearing," Smith draws a comparison between his congregation at St. Clement Danes and the ground; for they, like the ground, need to be "watered, and dressed, and

---

[40]Ibid.

manured" (1:333). In "The Trial of the Righteous," he compares God to a wasp. Although the wasp can sting but once, God has unlimited ability to sting us with "a generation of crosses and a plurality of troubles" (1:241). In "The Lawgiver's Answer," he compares God to a jealous husband who is "loath to have a partner in his love" (2:120). In both "The Godly Man's Request" and "The Christian Practice," he gives God a daughter, Wisdom, and compares God to a jealous, protective father who will not give his daughter to any man but "the man that loveth her, and sueth for her, and meaneth to set her at his heart" (1:286; cf. 1:253). In both "Jacob's Ladder" and "Mary's Choice," Christ undergoes a sexual metamorphosis, becoming our mother and giving us suck: "Christ which hath his breast full of heavenly milk, is glad when he hath children to suck the same" (2:361; cf. 2:85). Finally, we ourselves are metamorphosed in "The Affinity of the Faithful," becoming now Christ's mother, as he was ours in "Jacob's Ladder" and "Mary's Choice": we are Christ's mother; "every one which will have Christ his Saviour, must be Christ's mother" (2:295).

Many of the sermons are studded with quotable apothegms. Consistently his language is terse, clear, and to the point, and frequently his words fall into that happy collocation which turns them from the ordinary into the extraordinary, from merely clear to piercing, from general observations to universal truths. Following are some examples: "Seeing then your kingdom is not here, look not for a golden life in an iron world" (1:247); "It is easier for the bird to go by the net than to break the net; so it is easier for a man to avoid temptations than to overcome temptations" (1:299); "A man may go into a labyrinth easily; but when he is in he cannot get out" (1:307); "There is no way to escape sin, but to avoid occasion" (1:299); "So we are ashamed of sin, and yet not ashamed to sin" (1:418); "Sin is not remitted until the debt be restored" (1:107); "We see our sore, but not our salve" (1:237); "Now kill the serpent in the egg, for when he is a serpent he will kill thee" (1:223); "Such a schoolmaster is affliction, to teach that which prophets and angels cannot teach" (1:199); "A friend is never known before he be lost" (1:199); "Neither virtue nor vice goeth by age" (1:311); "That which teacheth one tempteth another" (1:306) and; "The golden mean is good for all things." (1:162)

Often Smith uses the rhetorical devices of parallelism, antithesis, and cataloging. A simple use of parallelism can be illustrated with a sentence on hypocrites from "The Christian's Sacrifice": "As easy to wring Hercules's club out of his fists, as to wring a penitent tear from their eyes, a faithful prayer from their lips, or a good thought from their heart" (1:120). Antithesis is evident in "The Young Man's Task" in a sentence concerning our delay in giving our lives to Christ: "When we were children, we deferred till we were men; when we are men, we defer till we be old men; when we are old men, we defer till death; in all our life we find no leisure to live well, but flit from sin to sin, from wicked speeches to wicked deeds, as the fly skippeth from scab to scab, until we be cast so far behind that we have no courage to go forward" (1:226). All three devices—antithesis, parallelism, and cataloging—can be seen in the following passage from "The Wedding Garment," concerning our putting on the armor of Christ Jesus:

> Faith is the hand which putteth him on. Faith taketh first his righteousness, and covereth her unrighteousness; then she taketh his obedience, and covereth her disobedience; then she taketh his patience, and covereth her impatience; then she taketh his temperance, and covereth her intemperance; then she taketh his continency, and covereth her incontinency; then she taketh his constancy, and covereth her inconstancy; then she taketh his faith, and covereth her diffidence; then she taketh his humility, and covereth her pride; then she taketh his love, and covereth her rancour; and so taketh one robe after another . . . until she have put on Jesus Christ. (1:149)

The tone of Smith's style, as John Lievsay observes, impresses the reader immediately with its "transparent sincerity and earnestness."[41] His tone is generally fatherly; when he reproves, he appears

[41]John L. Lievsay, " 'Silver-tongued Smith,' Paragon of Elizabethan

to be motivated by love. For instance, in "The Christian's Sacrifice," he sounds like a father pleading with his children.

> I wish you would give all your hearts to God while I speak, that ye might have a kingdom for them. Send for your hearts where they are wandering, one from the bank, another from the tavern, another from the shop, another from the theatres; call them home, and give them all to God, and see how he will welcome them, as the father embraceth the son. (1:124)

If, however, his usual tone is gentle, he can also be caustic and scolding. In his first sermon on "The Sweet Song of Old Father Simeon," he writes:

> I have somewhat to say to you of this parish. A dainty was prepared for you, and you let the strangers take it from you; you were required to a fast, and you did feast yourselves; you were required to come and pray unto the Lord, and to humble yourselves in his sight, that he may turn away his wrath from you; and you let the temple stand open and empty for your parts, and your shops were all open, and you were about your merchandise, forsaking God, and seeking to win the unjust mammon, and the vanities of the world. (2:179)

In "The Dialogue between Paul and King Agrippa," he scolds: "Thou which sayest thou art a Christian, hast rebelled more since thou rosest, than thou hast obeyed since thou wert born" (1:444).

Occasionally, his tone is philosophical: "Man is mortal, wisdom is immortal; yet by wisdom man becomes immortal too" (1:275); "It is safer eating with unwashed hands than with unwashed hearts" (1:70); "He which planted the vineyard is worthy to taste of the grape" (1:298); "When iniquity hath played her part, vengeance leaps upon the stage: the comedy is short, but the tragedy is longer" (2:324).

He achieves an especial poignancy when he writes on death. Consider the following sentences, all with their own epigrammatic force, taken from "The Godly Man's Request": "Everything every day suffers some eclipse, and nothing stands at a stay, but one

---

Preachers," *The Huntington Library Quarterly* 11 (November 1947) 14.

creature calls to another, 'Let us leave this world' " (1:279); "So many years as are past, so many years we are nearer to the last" (1:275); "Every man had need to die, to make him believe that he shall die" (1:278); "At last comes in *mortuus est,* that is, *he died,* which is the epitaph of every man" (1:278). In "The Fall of Nebuchadnezzar," he writes: "If we have but a week to repent, we will defer it to the last day, that we may sin all the rest" (1:186-87). He warns in "The Trumpet of the Soul," "Whilst the thief stealeth, the hemp groweth, and the hook is covered within the bait" (1:275).

Not only are the sermons themselves examples of Smith's masterful use of language, they also contain his own remarks on how words work. In "The Rebellion of Jonah," he comments on connotative meanings: "Words are not always to be taken as they properly signify, one thing is often spoken and another meant" (2:221). His own efforts, however, are always to clarify and to use language on its most literal level, as the Puritans generally insisted. In one instance, however, Smith is particularly insistent upon the use of language as symbol. In "A Treatise on the Lord's Supper," in which he argues against the Roman Catholic doctrine of transubstantiation, he writes: "It is the consent of all writers that a sacrament is a sign, therefore not the thing signified" (1:55). He points out that language is used symbolically in many instances. One might "call the prince a phoenix, the university a fountain, the court a peacock, the city a sea, the country a hermit" (1:55), and in all the instances everyone would immediately recognize the symbolic use of the language. He insists that the Catholics play the purist more than the Puritans when they refuse to see Christ's symbolic use of language at the Last Supper. He argues that it was "Christ's manner to teach by similitudes, shewing one thing by another, which is the plainest manner of teaching" (1:53); indeed, Smith employs Christ's method in his own sermons, in which he is constantly drawing comparisons between one thing and another. Those who believe in transubstantiation rest their belief, according to Smith, on Christ's words when he broke the bread at the Last

Supper: "This is my body." Those who take the sentence literally might, by the same fallacious logic, "Prove as well that Christ is a door, because he saith, 'I am the door,' . . . or a vine, because he saith, 'I am the vine' (1:47). "Why," argues Smith, "his body was not broken before he suffered; how did he say then, *which is broken*, before it was broken? There is no sense of it but this: bread was broken, and signified that his body should be." He warns:

> Figurative speeches must not be construed literally; but this is the heretics' fashion. If you mark, you shall see throughout that all the testimonies which the papists allege for their heresies, are either tropes, or figures, or allegories, or parables, or allusions, or dark speeches; which when they presume to expound allegorically, or literally, without conference of any other scriptures, then they wander and stray from the mark, or else it is impossible that the truth should maintain error, that is, that the Scriptures should speak for heresy, if it were not wrested and perverted; therefore we see that Eve never erred, until she corrupted the text, Gen. iii.3. (1:47-48)

Finally, in support of his argument against transubstantiation, he declaims emphatically on the nature of language as symbol:

> Again, for the figures to be turned into the thing signified by them, is utterly against the nature of a sacrament, and makes it no sacrament, because there is no sign; for every sacrament doth consist of a sign, and a thing signified: the sign is ever an earthly thing, and that which is signified is an heavenly thing. This shall appear in all examples: as, in paradise there was a very tree for the sign, and Christ the thing signified by it, Gen. ii.10; in circumcision there was a cutting off of the skin, and the cutting off of sin, Gen. xvii.11; in the passover there was a lamb, and Christ, Exod. xii.3; in the Sabbath there was a day of rest, and eternal rest, Exod. xxiii.11; in the sacrifices there was an offering of some beasts, and the offering of Christ, Heb. ix.1; in the sanctuary there was the holy place, and heaven, Exod. xxx; in the propitiatory there was a golden covering, and Christ our cover, Exod. xxv.24; in the wilderness there was a rock yielding water, and Christ yielding his blood, Exod. xvii.16; in the apparition there was a dove, and the Holy Ghost, Mat. iii.16; in the manna there was bread, and Christ, John vi.45; in baptism there is very water which washeth us, and Christ's blood

> washing us, John i.33; so in the supper of Christ there is very bread and wine for the sign, and the body and blood of Christ for the thing signified, 1 Cor. xi.26, or else this sacrament is against the nature of all other sacraments. (1:49)

Clearly, Smith is well skilled in the uses of language and can almost always find the right rhetorical device to achieve his desired effect. Alan Herr asserts that "Smith attacks the problems of rhetorical devices stolidly, as one who might say 'I shall preach fashionably though I choke in the attempt.' "[42] Herr is correct only in the sense that Smith seems always to be looking for the right word or comparison or device to illumine his language and message, but not in the sense that Smith yearns to preach fashionably. One who is acquainted with the sermons in their entirety is struck at once with his humility and general disregard for fashionable popularity.

His self-conscious use of language may perhaps be seen more clearly by observing a number of stylistic changes Smith made in two sermons which he borrowed from Thomas Bedel and Thomas Drant. Charactistically, he eliminates every Latin quotation from both sermons. He mentions the Church Fathers only sparingly, always identifying them with an appositive such as "Basil, an ancient father of the Church."[43] Usually, however, he drops the name entirely, replacing it with an expression like "A learned writer."[44] He freely manipulates Bedel's and Drant's language to achieve his own idea of clarity.

As Thomas Ehret has discovered, "If one compares syntax in the following passages [between Drant and Smith], he sees at once that Smith's is easier to follow":[45]

---

[42]Alan Fager Herr, *The Elizabethan Sermon,* p. 100.

[43]Thomas K. Ehret, *Four Sermons of Henry Smith*, p. lxi. For a full examination of Smith's debt to Thomas Bedel and Thomas Drant, see Ehret, pp. lx-lxvii.

[44]Ibid.

[45]Ibid., pp. lxiii-lxiv.

> *DRANT*
> We may see like wise a president of our punishment for not giving almes. In that ritch personne which St. Luke speaketh of, Chapter 16. The which ritch man after his death, to his greater graefe sae Lazarus whom he had contemned, in one hauen of rest with Abraham.
>
> *SMITH*
> There are many rich persons, that thinke scorne to releue the pore, of whose hard dealing we haue a president in the sixteenth of *Luke*: The rich man in his lifetime woulde not releue *Lazarus*, but despised him; yea, he forgot God, and thought there was no God (but his gold) that cold in justice punishe him, for despising the poore. *Lazarus* died for want, and so did *Diues* for all his wealth; who soone after (being in hell) beheld *Lazarus* in heauen, triumphing in *Abrahams* bosome, while hee was tormented in hell fire.

Ehret discloses a number of other examples which Smith takes from the sermons of Drant and Bedel, always changing them for his own purposes. In each case, he reshapes the language of the original in order to communicate its message more clearly.

In "The True Trial of the Spirits," Smith sums up his own view of the joining of matter and manner and to what end they are to be joined:

> There is a kind of preachers risen up but of late, which shroud and cover every rustical, and unsavoury, and childish, and absurd sermon, under the name of the simple kind of teaching, like the popish priests, which make ignorance the mother of devotion; but indeed, to preach simply is not to preach rudely, nor unlearnedly, nor confusedly, but to preach plainly and perspicuously, that the simplest man may understand what is taught, as if he did hear his name. (1:139)

Because he desires so earnestly to be understood by all his hearers, he is, as John L. Lievsay observes, "wary of figures which depart very far from the literal and the concrete. Allegory, symbolism, and the involved analogy are virtually absent from his sermons."[46] Also,

---

[46]John L. Lievsay, "*Silver-tongued Smith,*" p. 26-27.

as Lievsay notes, Smith, for the same reason, frequently repeats the central points of his sermon, generally preceding them by stock expressions like the following from "A Preparative to Marriage": "Because I have spoken more than you can remember, if you ask me what is most needful to bear away, in my opinion, there is one saying of Paul which is the profitablest sentence in all the Scripture for man and wife to meditate often" (1:39). In his second sermon on "A Treatise on the Lord's Supper," he writes, "Now we come to that examination, which is the epitome or abridgment of all these" (1:82). Later, in the same sermon, he urges, "Now if you cannot remember all that I have said, yet remember the text" (1:84). Such summations are characteristic of the sermons and reflect Smith's desire that his congregation grasp the central point of his message.

Overall, Smith strives to unite the force of language with the force of thought, and to a great degree he is highly successful. He joins matter and manner in a happy union, presenting the Christian doctrine, as he understands it, with simplicity and force. In a vigorous, lucid style, which permits his sermons to be read with ease and pleasure some four centuries later, he tells the Christian story over and over again—the story of Jesus, of his crucifixion, his resurrection, his ascension, his gift of eternal life to mankind. Although he may not deserve to be ranked among the very greatest preachers, he is, nevertheless, worthy of admiration. In an age respected for its sermons, Smith achieved a notable popularity. Not only in his own time, but also in succeeding ages, his sermons have won and have deserved to win the approbation of discerning judges. They are the monument to his memory, insuring that, whenever English sermons are talked of, Henry Smith's will be mentioned with admiration and respect.

Bibliography

Ames, Joseph. *Typographical Antiquities: or An Historical Account of the Origin and Progress of Printing in Great Britain and Ireland: containing Memoirs of Our Ancient Printers, and a Register of Books Printed by Them from the Year 1471 to the Year 1600*. Edited by William Herbert. 3 vols. London, 1785.

Aquinas, St. Thomas. *Summa Theologia*. Translated by Fathers of the English Dominican Province. New York: Benziger Brothers, Inc., 1947.

Ayre, John, ed. *The Sermons of Edwin Sandys, D.D.* Cambridge: Cambridge University Press, 1841.

———. *The Works of John Jewel, Bishop of Salisbury*. Cambridge: Cambridge University Press, 1847.

Baily, John Eglington. *The Life of Thomas Fuller, D.D., with Notices of His Books, His Kinsmen, and His Friends*. London: Basil Montagu Pickering, 1874.

Blench, J. W. *Preaching in England in the late Fifteenth and Sixteenth Centuries: A Study of English Sermons 1450-c.1600*. Oxford: Basil Blackwell, 1964.

Brook, Benjamin. *The Lives of the Puritans: Containing a Biographical Account of those Divines Who Distinguished Themselves in the Cause of Religious Liberty, from the Reformation under Queen Elizabeth to the Act of Uniformity, in 1662*. 3 vols. London: Printed for James Black, 1813.

Bruce, John, ed. *Diary of John Manningham, of the Middle Temple, and of Bradbourne, Kent, Barrister-at-Law, 1602-1603*. Edited from the original manuscript and presented to the Camden Society by William Tite. Westminster: Printed by J. B. Nichols and Sons, 1868.

Burton, William. *The Description of Leicester Shire, Containing Matters of Antiquitye, Historye, Armorye, and Genealogy*. London: Printed for John White, 1622.

Bush, Douglas. *English Literature in the Earlier Seventeenth Century 1600-1660*. New York: Oxford University Press, 1952.

Chalmers, Alexander, ed. *The General Biographical Dictionary, Containing an Historical and Critical Account of the Lives and Writings of the Most Eminent Persons in Every Nation; Particularly the British and Irish; from the Earliest Accounts to the Present Time.* London, 1816.

Collinson, Patrick. *The Elizabethan Puritan Movement.* Berkeley and Los Angeles CA: University of California Press, 1967.

Cooper, Charles Henry and Thompson Cooper, comps. *Athenae Cantabrigienses.* Cambridge: Deighton, Bell, and Co., 1861.

———. "Henry Smith, Lecturer of St. Clement Danes," *Notes and Queries.* 2nd series. vol. 8, 20 August 1859. London: Bell & Daldy, 1859.

Cooper, Thompson. "The Early Use of Shorthand," *Notes and Queries.* 8th series. vol. 10, 5 September 1896. London: John C. Francis, Bream's Buildings, Chancery Lane, 1896.

Davies, Horton. *Worship and Theology in England from Cranmer to Hooker, 1534-1603.* 5 vols. Princeton NJ: Princeton University Press, 1970.

Deane, Herbert A. *The Political and Social Ideas of St. Augustine.* New York: Columbia University Press, 1963.

Devereux, James A., S. J. "The Collects of the First *Book of Common Prayer* as Works of Translation," *Studies in Philology* 66:5 (1969).

———. "The Primers and the Prayer Book Collects," *Huntington Library Quarterly* 32 (1968).

———. "Reformed Doctrine in the First *Book of Common Prayer,*" *Harvard Theological Review* 58 (1965).

Ehret, Thomas King. *Four Sermons of Henry Smith: A Critical Edition.* Dissertation, University of Illinois, Urbana IL, 1968.

Emerson, Everett H. *English Puritanism from John Hooper to John Milton.* Durham NC: Duke University Press, 1968.

Foster, Joseph, comp. *Alumni Oxonienses: The Members of the University of Oxford, 1500-1714: Their Parentage, Birthplace, and Year of Birth, with a Record of Their Degrees.* Oxford: James Parker & Co., 1891.

Fox, Arthur W. *A Book of Bachelors.* New York: E. P. Dutton and Co.; Westminster: Archibald Constable and Co., 1900.

Fuller, Thomas. *The Church History of Britain: From the Birth of Jesus Christ, Until the Year M.DC.XLVIII.* London: Printed for John Williams at the sign of the Crown in St. Paul's Church-yard, 1655.

———. *The Church History of Britain; from The Birth of Jesus Christ until the Year M.DC.XLVIII.* Edited by J. S. Brewer. 6 vols. Oxford University Press, 1845.

———. *The History of the Worthies of England.* Edited by P. Austin Nuttall. 3 vols. London: Printed for Thomas Tegg by Nuttall and Hodgson, Gough Square, 1840.

Garrett, Christina Hallowell. *The Marian Exiles: A Study in the Origins of Elizabethan Puritanism.* Cambridge: Cambridge University Press, 1938.

George, Charles H. and Katherine. *The Protestant Mind of the English Reformation 1570-1640.* Princeton: Princeton University Press, 1961.

Gordon, Sir Adam, ed. *Discourses on Several Subjects: Being the Substance of the Homilies of the Church of England.* 2nd ed. 2 vols. London: Printed by S. Gosmell, Little Queen Street, for Ogles, Duncan, and Cochran, 37 Paternoster Row, and 295 Holborn; J. Ogle, Edinburgh; M. Ogle, Glasgow; and T. Johnston, Dublin, 1817.

Granger, J., comp. *A Biographical History of England from Egbert the Great to the Revolution.* 3 vols. London: Printed for T. Davies, in Russel-Street, Covent-Garden, 1769.

Hall, Edwin. *The Puritans and Their Principles.* 3rd ed. New York: Baker and Scribner, 1847.

Haller, William. *Liberty and Reformation in the Puritan Revolution.* New York: Columbia University Press, 1955; reprinted 1963.

________. *The Rise of Puritanism; Or, The Way to the New Jerusalem as Set Forth in Pulpit and Press from Thomas Cartwright to John Lilburne and John Milton, 1570-1643.* New York: Columbia University Press, 1938; reprinted Philadelphia: University of Pennsylvania Press, 1972.

Hargrave, Francis, ed. *A Complete Collection of State-Trials for High-Treason, and Other Crimes and Misdemeanours; Commencing with the Eleventh Year of the Reign of King Richard II and Ending with the Sixteenth Year of the Reign of King George III.* 4th ed. London: Printed by T. Wright for C. Bathurst and sold by G. Kearsly, 1776.

Henson, H. Hensley, D.D. *Puritanism in England.* New York: Burt Franklin, 1972.

Herr, Alan Fager. *The Elizabethan Sermon: A Survey and a Bibliography.* Dissertation, University of Pennsylvania, Philadelphia PA, 1940.

Hunter, Joseph. *New Illustrations of the Life, Studies, and Writings of Shakespeare.* 2 vols. London: J. B. Nichols and Son, 1845.

Jewel, John. *An Apology of the Church of England.* Edited by J. E. Booty. Ithaca NY, 1963.

Kirby, Ethyn Williams. *William Prynne: A Study in Puritanism.* Cambridge MA: Harvard University Press, 1931.

Knappen, M. M. *Tudor Puritanism: A Chapter in the History of Idealism.* Gloucester MA: Peter Smith, 1963.

Krapp, George Philip. *The Rise of English Literary Prose.* New York: Frederick Ungar Publishing Co., 1915; republished 1963.

Lewis, C. S. *English Literature in the Sixteenth Century Excluding Drama.* Oxford: The Clarendon Press, 1944.

Lievsay, John L. " 'Silver-tongued Smith,' Paragon of Elizabethan Preachers," *The Huntington Library Quarterly* 11 (November 1947).

Maclure, Millar. *The Paul's Cross Sermons: 1534-1642.* Toronto, Canada: University of Toronto Press, 1958.

Mair, G. H., ed. *Wilson's Arte of Rhetorique, 1560.* Oxford: The Clarendon Press, 1909.

Mallett, Charles Edward. A *History of the University of Oxford.* 2 vols. New York: Longmans, Green and Co., 1924.

Marsden, J. B. *The History of the Early Puritans from the Reformation to the Opening of the Civil War in 1642.* London: Hamilton, Adams, & Co., 1850.

May, G. Lacey, ed. *An Anthology of Caroline Preachers with 60 Extracts from their Sermons.* London: S.P.C.K., 1955.

McKerrow, Ronald B., ed. *The Works of Thomas Nashe.* 5 vols. Reprinted from the original edition with corrections and supplementary notes by F. P. Wilson. Oxford: Basil Blackwell, 1958.

Milward, Peter. *Shakespeare's Religious Background.* Bloomington: Indiana University Press, 1973.

Mitchell, W. Fraser. *English Pulpit Oratory from Andrewes to Tillotson: A Study of Its Literary Aspects.* London: Society for Promoting Christian Knowledge, 1932.

Nash, Thomas. *Pierce Penniless's Supplication to the Devil.* Edited by J. Payne Collier from the First Edition of 1592. London: Reprinted for the Shakespeare Society by F. Shoberl, 1842.

Neal, Daniel. *The History of the Puritans, or Protestant Nonconformists, from the Reformation in 1517, to the Revolution in 1688.* 2 vols. New York: Harper & Brothers, 1844.

Nichols, John. *The History and Antiquities of the County of Leicester.* London: Printed by and for Nichols, Son, and Bentley, 1795.

Phillimore, John George. *History of England during the Reign of George the Third.* London: Virtue Brothers & Co., 1863.

Pierce, William. *An Historical Introduction to the Marprelate Tracts: A Chapter in the Evolution of Religions and Civil Liberty in England.* London: Archibald Constable & Co., Ltd., 1908.

Pollard, Arthur. *English Sermons.* London: Longmans, Green & Co., 1963.

Pollock, Frederick, ed. *Table Talk of John Selden.* London, 1927.

Quarles, Frances. *Divine Fancies Digested into Epigrammes, Meditations, and Observations.* London: Printed by M. F. for John Marriot, 1641.

Richardson, Caroline Francis. *English Preachers and Preaching 1640-1670.* New York: The Macmillan Company, 1928.

Seaver, Paul S. *The Puritan Lectureships: The Politics of Religious Dissent 1560-1662.* Stanford CA: Stanford University Press, 1970.

Simpson, W. Sparrow. *Chapters in the History of Old S. Paul's.* London: Elliot Stock, 1881.

Smith, Thomas, ed. *The Works of Henry Smith.* 2 vols. Edinburgh: James Nichol, 1866.

Stephen, Sir Leslie and Sir Sidney Lee, eds. *The Dictionary of National Biography: From the Earliest Times to 1900.* London: Geoffrey Cumberlege. Printed at the Oxford University Press 1921-1922 from plates furnished by Messrs. Spottiswoode & Co. and again 1937-1938, 1949-1950.

Strype, John. *Annals of the Reformation and Establishment of Religion, and Other Various Occurences in the Church of England, during Queen Elizabeth's Happy Reign.* 4 vols. Oxford: The Clarendon Press, 1824.

———. *Historical Collections of the Life and Acts of the Right Reverend Father in God, John Aylmer, Lord Bp. of London in the Reign of Queen Elizabeth.* Oxford: The Clarendon Press, 1821.

Tanner, Thomas. *Bibliotheca Britannico-Hibernica: sive, de Scriptoribus, qui in Anglia, Scotia, et Hibernia ad saeculi XVII initium floruerunt, literarum ordine juxta familiarum nomina dispositis Commentarius.* London: William Bowyer, 1748.

Tillyard, E. M. W. *The Elizabethan World Picture.* London: Chatto & Windus, 1950.

Venn, John and J. A. Venn, comps. *Alumni Cantabrigienses: A Biographical List of All Known Students, Graduates and Holders of Office at the University of Cambridge, from the Earliest Times to 1900.* Cambridge: Cambridge University Press, 1927.

Ward, Sir A. W. and A. R. Waller, eds. *The Cambridge History of English Literature.* 15 vols. Cambridge: Cambridge University Press, 1961.

White, Helen C. *Social Criticism in Popular Religious Literature of the Sixteenth Century.* New York: The Macmillan Company, 1944.

Willey, Basil. *The Seventeenth Century Background: Studies in the Thought of the Age in Relation to Poetry and Religion.* London: Chatto & Windus, 1934. Reprinted, New York: Columbia University Press, 1952.

Wood, Anthony A., comp. *Athenae Oxonienses: An Exact History of All the Writers and Bishops Who Have Had Their Education in the University of Oxford: To Which Is Added the Fasti, or Annals of the Said University: A New Edition, with Additions, and a Continuation,* ed. Philip Bliss. London: T. Bensley, Printer, Bolt Court, Fleet Street, 1815.

Index

HENRY SMITH: ENGLAND'S SILVER-TONGUED PREACHER

Designed by Haywood Ellis

Composition was by Omni Composition Services, Macon, Georgia
typeface—Weiss
the text was "read" by a Hendrix Typereader II OCR Scanner
and formatted by Janet Middlebrooks on an Addressograph Multigraph
Comp/Set 5404, then paginated on an A/M Comp/Set 4510.

Production specifications:
text paper—60 pound Warren's Olde Style
endpapers—Process Materials Corporation Multicolor Antique, scarlet
cover (on .088 boards)—Holliston Roxite B 51502, stamped with Colorit 914
and jacket—100 pound offset enamel, printed two colors (PMS 484 burgundy
and PMS 134 cream) and varnished

Printing (offset lithography) was by Omnipress of Macon, Inc., Macon, Georgia
Binding was by John H. Dekker and Sons, Inc., Grand Rapids, Michigan